Gospel Opportunity
or
Gospel Threat?

GOSPEL OPPORTUNITY OR GOSPEL THREAT?

THE CHURCH'S DEBATE ON SEXUALITY

By
GRAY TEMPLE
DIANE KNIPPERS
JAMES STANTON
LOUIE CREW

Foreword by Peter Lee

 CHURCH

Church Publishing Incorporated, New York

Library of Congress Cataloging-in-Publication Data

Gospel opportunity or gospel threat? : the church's debate on
    sexuality / Gray Temple . . . [et al.].
            p.   cm.
    Papers presented at conferences established by the Virginia Diocesan
Center as a memorial to the Right Reverend Robert F. Gibson, Jr.
    Includes bibliographical references.
    ISBN 0-89869-311-X (pbk.)
    1. Homosexuality–Religious aspects–Episcopal Church–Congresses.
2. Ordination of gays–Religious aspects–Episcopal Church–Congresses.
3. Same-sex marriage–Religious aspects–Episcopal Church–Congresses.
4. Episcopal Church–Doctrines–Congresses.
I. Temple, Gray, 1941–   .
BX5979.5.H65G67 1998   98-51352
261.8' 35766–dc21   CIP

Church Publishing Incorporated
445 Fifth Avenue
New York NY 10016

5 4 3 2 1

CONTENTS

EDITOR'S NOTE

The following material is transcribed from audiotapes of the third Burning Issues Conference: "Gospel Opportunity or Gospel Threat? The Church's Debate on Sexuality." Peter Lee, Bishop of Virginia, acted as moderator of the conference, which was attended by a standing-room-only audience of 110 people. Participants other than the four listed speakers are not identified in the text. Question and answer segments have been edited for continuity

The order of presentation was chosen by lot. Each speaker was allotted 45 minutes for a presentation and questions from the audience. The final 45-minute session was a panel discussion, including questions from the audience, which were presented by Peter Lee, who frequently condensed a number of similar questions into a single one.

We are grateful for the cooperation of the staff of the Diocese of Virginia and the Virginia Diocesan Center at Roslyn for their assistance in the production of this book.

FOREWORD

Put yourself in the position of members of the church 100 years from now. How will they regard our contemporary sexuality debate? First, I suspect they will wonder what all the fuss was about. No one can predict with certainty what the future will bring. It may be foolhardy, but I will risk an attempt. I believe our spiritual descendants will continue to regard marriage as a sign of the union between Christ and Christ's church; that God's powerful gift of sexuality will be respected by the values of marriage instructing us on the exercise of sexual expression. I believe that with a century's greater knowledge of the diversity of human sexual orientation, Christian marriage will inform other commitments that are based on the church's traditional covenant of marriage. That means continuity with the past. That means faithfulness with Scripture, and that means adaptations that may well lead to acceptance of covenants between persons of the same sex without any sense of betrayal of what the church has taught for centuries.

If that future scenario is possible or desirable, how do we get there? I believe that we will arrive at that point through prayerful and serious engagement with one another, which includes conflict and debate. For Christians, conflict and debate within a loving community means seeking the Truth that is in Jesus, seeking that truth together, and not excluding those with whom we disagree.

The 1997 Burning Issues Conference dealt with, "Gospel Opportunity or Gospel Threat? The Church's Debate on Sexuality." The speakers represented a variety of thoughtful reflections, some of which are clearly in conflict, but what was evident at the conference was a seriousness of faith and a seriousness of commitment to discern God's truth faithfully and obediently.

The Burning Issues Conference was established by the Virginia Diocesan Center as a memorial to the Right Reverend Robert F. Gibson, Jr., who was Bishop of the Diocese of Virginia from 1960 until he retired in 1974. He died in 1990.

Bishop Gibson was an outspoken, compassionate seeker after God's truth in public life, especially in matters of racial justice and in areas of church unity. He understood the necessity of seeking both truth and unity. He was an advocate and witness in the prime of his ministry in the 1960s and early 1970s. And this Burning Issues Conference is held in thankful memory for his ministry.

The first conference was on Racism, the second on End of Life Issues—assisted suicide, care of the dying—and the subject of the third Burning Issues Conference was the sexuality debate.

Each of the four presenters whose paper is reproduced here is a loyal and faithful Christian and an active Episcopalian, involved in the life of the church at the local, diocesan and national level. The sequence of the presentations was chosen by lot.

I am grateful to Church Publishing Incorporated for making available the papers of the conference for the wider church as we engage in a church-wide debate. The Burning Issues Conference began with this prayer from the Book of Common Prayer that I pray will continue to inform and guide us as we seek God's unfolding truth:

> O God, you have bound us together in a common life. Help us, in the midst of our struggles for justice and truth, to confront one another without hatred or bitterness, and to work together with mutual forbearance and respect; through Jesus Christ Our Lord. Amen.

Peter James Lee
Bishop of Virginia
October 1998

CHAPTER I

TALKING ABOUT SEX
The Structure of the Argument

by GRAY TEMPLE

Gray Temple was ordained deacon and priest in 1968 in the Diocese of Western North Carolina, assigned to St. Luke's Church in Boone and as Episcopal Campus Minister to Appalachian State University. He became Rector of St. Patrick's, Atlanta, in 1975.

Understanding its purpose as "Worship, Fellowship, and Ministry," St. Patrick's has become one of the conspicuously vibrant worship centers in the church. It has developed a system of internal cohesion (cell groups) to maintain intimacy in the face of its size. Under Gray Temple's leadership, the congregation has heroically weathered controversies of parish identity, a painful staff upheaval, and a controversy over the sacramental status of homosexual Christians, emerging from each with buoyant energy and sharpened vision. (For a sense of the latter, consult "The Rector's Vision" on the St. Patrick's Webpage :http://www.netdepot.com/~stpatric/.)

Gray Temple has served the Diocese of Atlanta in key capacities, including service as president of the Standing Committee. Outside the parish, Gray's ministry consists largely of teaching and consultation. This has taken him across Asia, to Africa (where he is an honorary Canon of St. Luke's Cathedral in Butere, Kenya), to Europe, and across this country. As a member of S.O.M.A./USA (Sharing Ministries Abroad), Gray conducted a teaching mission in Zaire, narrowly escaping as a refugee as the country collapsed. He has led group study excursions to the Holy Lands, to Turkey, and to Kenya.

Gray Temple married Jean Dillin Temple in 1966. They have two sons.

I would like us to begin by praying for each other, by congratulating God for each other.

> O God of peace, who hast taught us that in returning and rest we shall be saved, in quietness and in confidence shall be our strength: By the might of thy Spirit lift us, we pray thee, to thy presence, where we may be still and know that thou art God; through Jesus Christ our Lord. Amen.

There's a cartoon on the wall of my office: A bailiff is swearing in a supercilious-looking academic, saying, "Do you swear to tell the truth, the whole truth, and nothing but the truth—and not in some sneaky, relativistic way?" I'll try to comply with that oath this evening.

It's tempting to evade the actual topic that draws us together. The topic was carefully worded: "Gospel Opportunity or Gospel Threat? 1The Church's Debate on Sexuality."

While I feel an enormous tug to get into the substance of the debate that wracks the church right now, I also feel it important to take this opportunity to stand back and look at the debate itself. Therefore, I'm not going to get very much into the substance of whether we should solemnize same-sex unions or whether people who are in committed same-sex unions are a sufficiently wholesome example to the flock of Christ that they should be ordained to the diaconate, the priesthood and the episcopate. However, I wish to make it clear at the outset that I am very much in favor of the solemnization of same-sex unions and I believe that there are any number of people in committed, same-sex relationships who are wholesome examples to the flock of Christ. But, rather than try to persuade you of that, what I'd like to do is to talk about how we talk about sexuality in the church. Our presence here, our interest in this topic, and the fact that this conference is sold out, indicates to me that we are involved in a conflict in the Episcopal Church, a conflict in which we all have a very high stake.

First, let me discuss conflict itself. The most important thing we know about conflict is that no conflict is resoluble at the level at which is waged. There are any number of examples of this. The war in Bosnia goes back nine hundred years. Military defeat, unless it kills the enemy, doesn't silence him and doesn't silence his family. According to Jacques Ellul, we didn't win anything in World War II, because the Nazi spirit now governs our economies and people are economic ciphers, not human beings. If I had a fight with my wife this afternoon before I left the house, and walked away thinking I won it, any husband here can tell me the fight is not over.

St. Paul tells us in Romans, Chapter 7: 14-25 that every one of us is a walking civil war, caught in the struggle between our internal impulses on the one hand and the law on the other hand. And there is no good place in the spectral tension between those two. There is no place of comfort.

We don't resolve that conflict by weakening the law so we can indulge our impulses, nor do we resolve it by tightening the law, so that it squashes our impulses. In Romans, Chapter 8:11, we are told to imagine what we would do if the Spirit that raised the body of Jesus Christ in the tomb got hold of us right this minute. We have a picture of the Holy Spirit lifting us to a higher place where we can be still and know not only that God is God, but that we are God's own. And from that place we can look down at the conflict and, in the loving embrace of God, chuckle at it. That's how we resolve our internal tension.

Something like that is necessary for the church on this terribly important issue of sexuality. I am not very well versed in the secular expression of this debate, but the little I've read about it makes me proud to be a Christian. My sense is that in the church we do a little better job of talking about this than they do in the law courts or in various secular journals. And even there, the best voices tend to be those of Christians.

However, that's not saying much, because each of us knows that we really aren't very far along in this discussion. We are at something of an impasse that we are reacting to by sub-dividing into communities of agreement; we wear little partisan ribbons in our lapels so we can spot each other. We expend our energies, primarily, in the maintenance of the plausibility of our own positions. The notion is that of plausibility maintenance, discussed by Peter Berger in his books, *The Social Construction of Reality* and *The Sacred Canopy*. And for the most part, we preach to the choir and make sure our side has the glibbest take on things, rather than spend our time and our energy in prayer, or in prayerful, mutual, fresh exploration. We have not found each other's arguments persuasive. As a matter of fact, at lunch today, Bishop Stanton and I were chuckling over the fact that each of the four speakers on the program for this conference could probably write each other's speeches—we have heard all the arguments on both sides, but that has made no difference.

Not only have we not embraced each other's arguments, but we resent each other's insults. I'm heartily sick of them. As a liberal, I very much dislike being called a revisionist. I dislike the inference that somehow I'm involved in this debate because I'm trying to cloak my own secret sexual sins. And I'll bet those of you who disagree with me on this issue don't like being called homophobic. In fact, I daresay, there's not a homophobe in this room. I'll also bet you dislike being called reactionary, that you resent the inference that your zeal on this issue masks your secret sexual sins, and that you dislike being called developmentally challenged.

Furthermore, the metaphors that we've used in argument with each other have not proven persuasive. I don't think the metaphors that we liberals have used to persuade some of you have served any of us very well. I am quite sympathetic with those conservatives who stop me when I compare the struggle for gay rights in the church to the civil rights struggle. There are common elements, but notice what that metaphor does—it says, "Just as the white conservatives were wrong, you are wrong." And that front-loads the conclusion into the premise; that's "sneaky and relativistic."

I also deeply agree with Bishop John Howe of Florida, who recently made the point, originally posited by Bishop William Frey, that if you take the traditional sexual morality of the church and say, "This is going to be the initial thesis in a Hegelian dialectic," you have guaranteed that you're not going to wind up with the traditional teaching of the church. That's dishonest. Anyone familiar with Hegel can feel it. And though I may find that approach personally persuasive, it's dirty arguing. "Sneaky and relativistic."

And as a liberal, I would just as soon that you spare us the comparison of homosexuality to alcoholism. Drunkenness has never yet been a means of grace, anywhere, to anybody. But some of us are asking you to examine the claim that some same-sex unions are means of grace. And if you compare those relationships to alcoholism, you've front-loaded the notion that grace is an impossibility into the very beginning of the argument. And that is a sneaky, relativistic way of saying homosexuality is a toxic, socially corrosive disease. We need different metaphors, we need different comparisons, and we need different figures of speech.

Let's stop doing that to each other.

There are questions I'd love to discuss temperately with people who disagree with my wish to marry and ordain suitable people involved in same-sex unions. For example, the arguments I've seen insisting that homosexuality is corrosive of families strike me as logically circular, tautological; I'd be interested to hear a deeper discussion. Or the reading strategies by which homosexuality gets privileged attention over other sexual teachings, which we routinely ignore or reject. But this is not the setting—though my room might be later on—over a glass of Scotch.

What we *can* do in this setting is re-examine how we've conducted the discussion in recent years, recognizing that our lack of resolution is built into the structure of the conversation itself: adversarial processes are inherently irresoluble. We can search for ways that the Holy Spirit might fulfill Jesus' high priestly prayer: "That they all might be one. . . ." (John 17:21)

Did he mean, "That they might keep their institutional identities intact; that they might hold one opinion on every matter"? Some days I act as though he did. Or was he praying that whoever the proto-Quakers were who produced the Johannine Epistles might share grace with whoever the proto-Catholics were who wrote the Pastoral Epistles—without having to change a word they'd written? That Paul and James might praise God for each other—and mean it?

I want to propose another metaphorical framework, taking advantage of an area in which the church is already at work— the Ecumenical Movement. At the last General Convention, Ecumenism and the sacramental status of gay and lesbian Episcopalians were the two burning issues.

Let me tell you what these seemingly disparate issues have in common. The Ecumenical Movement really started in the Episcopal Church in the 1880s when William Reed Huntington developed the Chicago-Lambeth Quadrilateral. That document established the basis on which Episcopalians have conducted ecumenical discussions for about a century. The Quadrilateral comprises four points on the basis of which Anglicans are willing to discuss church union with any Christian group. And they're wonderful points.

[W]e account the following, to wit:

1. The Holy Scriptures of the Old and New Testament as the revealed Word of God.
2. The Nicene Creed as sufficient statement of the Christian Faith.
3. The two Sacraments,—Baptism and the Supper of the Lord,—ministered with unfailing use of Christ's words of institution and of the elements ordained by Him.
4. The Historic Episcopate, locally adapted in the methods of its administration to the varying needs of the nations and peoples called of God into the unity of His Church. (BCP, '79: pp. 876-877)

Most Christian groups share three of those four quadrilateral elements. There's really no debate about the first three.

Despite widespread agreement on the first three elements, the Quadrilateral got no takers. It was that fourth element—bishops in the Apostolic Succession—that repelled others. Other denominations (rightly) replied, "These Anglicans have put nothing on the table really. They are willing to join with any who will become Anglicans!" Subsequent phrasings and presentations have attempted to sweeten that element, but nobody is buying—most recently the Evangelical Lutheran Church in America (ELCA). I pray that the Lutherans do not rush to union with us until we resolve that this is not to be a morganatic marriage, that is, a marriage between two permanent unequals.

To get serious attention from other Christian groups, we will have to be willing to say something like this:

"We who have received grace through the Apostolic Ministry are eager to share that grace with those who have received grace through other ministries. . . ." But we'll have to go one terrifying step further: ". . . and are eager to have you share the grace of your ministry with us."

That's scary. It makes part of me want to fight. I clutch up when thinking of ecumenism with Presbyterians: we might have to replace the bishop's cathedra in my sanctuary with a rack for folding chairs, representing their (grace-filled) Episcopate-by-Committee!

To do ecumenism honestly will cost us something in historical identity—and the result is by no means guaranteed or clear. All of us in this room are caught between two contrary values: the grace that Anglicanism embodies, and our Lord's deepest wish: "That they might all be one. . . ."

At present that feels like the choice we must make. If God is not in the room with us, that choice will always be a tug-of-war, adversarial, irresoluble interdenominational name-calling. The only thing that will get us and the Lutherans and others over the hump to agreeing with Jesus is if we compare graces. (Grace: real and palpable—the discernible impact of the Spirit's work, the transforming presence of Jesus.) Alternative visions of unity may emerge, visions that do not require abdicating core values. But they cannot emerge until we talk at the level of grace we have received.

I once heard a Roman priest ask a large gathering, "Can you think of a single righteous use of the term 'non-Catholic'?" He was onto something, I think.

When Baptists reproach us for infant Baptism by sprinkling, we waste God's good oxygen by arguing back. What we must do is praise God right then for the received grace that makes them so excited about adult-believer Baptism—and beg them to share it with us.

Like participants in ecumenical discussion, all of us here debating the sacramental standing of homosexual Christians share most values in common. All four of us are saved; all know Jesus personally. All four of us treasure the enrichment of our marriages provided by sexual fidelity and decorum. And all of us have received grace through the positions we espouse. May we share that grace with each other? May we request it of each other?

And most of you here share most important core values. Specifically, most of you have given your lives to Jesus Christ at some point. Some of you, including me, have asked God's Holy Spirit to animate us. We have that much in common. We have in common the deep, abiding, grateful thanksgiving to God the Holy Spirit, who makes us faithful to our partners sexually and emotionally so that our intimate relationships can bear fruit.

Would those of you who oppose gay unions and the ordination of people in committed same-sex relations expose me to the grace you enjoy in that belief? (I'm quite familiar with your position's capacity to punish. Spare me.)

We are grace-receivers too, through what we believe. We have received grace through the positions we espouse and I think it would be glorious if we could spend our time together sharing the grace we receive through the positions we represent and the communities who help to reinforce those beliefs. I ask this quite seriously. I'm well familiar with the punishment that can come from such circles. But I'd love to feel some of the grace. I'm tired of punishing people who disagree with me; I'd love a chance to share with some of you the grace of where I believe God has brought me.

I'd love to share with you the grace Jesus has offered me as he has turned me inside out on this matter. (I promise to spare you the toxic opprobrium that my perspective so often sprays onto those we disagree with. You're already quite familiar with it.)

If we could do that, let me start out by recounting a couple of episodes where I think I received grace from God. They have much to do with why I occupy my present understanding.

Louie Crew and I have been friends for twenty years. It started with an argument that Louie, because he is a gracious Christian, refused to let become a quarrel. It took many years before that witness and the witness of so many of his colleagues finally got to me and I realized that these people are telling me the truth, these people are the same kind of thing as I am. Still it took a long time before God got to me and said, "It's really time for you to change your mind."

The first I knew this was happening was in the early summer of 1991, just before General Convention. We were doing an adult Sunday school presentation on issues that would come before the Convention. I was at my prayers. I think it was on a Tuesday, because I had to give a lecture to the adults on Sunday and I was going to present the traditional Episcopal approach that sex of any kind is to be confined to marriage; consequently this excludes sexually active homosexuals from ministry. I was praying that I would be able to present that well, and I think what I meant by well was without getting my tail feathers scorched.

And God did what God sometimes does. God interrupted the prayer. And I heard the interruption as a question. The question was: "If I wanted to introduce the grace of relational stability to my homosexual children and I wanted the church to help me with that by making the sacrament of Holy Matrimony available to them, is there a church in America that could hear me make that request?" That was all.

The implicit answer was, "No. Liberal churches might do it, but we'd do it as a publicity stunt, not because God told us to." Conservative churches would not believe it was God. They'd think they were being deceived by the devil. The answer was, "No. God cannot be heard to make that request."

God didn't say, "Gray, I want you to go do it, or I'm about to tell the church to do it," but the possibility got raised for the first time. That never happened to me before.

A few months later I was out west with friend of mine, a graduate of Trinity School of Ministry in Ambridge, Pennsylvania, who's much more conservative than I am. I was telling him about this experience and he said, "Man, that's wild. Something like that happened to me."

"How?" I asked.

He said, "Well, I was praying at that General Convention about this issue and all of a sudden the Lord called Matthew, Chapter 16 to mind, 'I will give you the keys of the kingdom of heaven, and whatever you bind on earth will be bound in heaven, and whatever you loose on earth will be loosed in heaven.'"

My friend went on, "And God asked, 'Why are you so chicken-hearted with that power? If you were to decide that these relationships could be solemnized, don't you think I'd back that?'"

And I said, "Do you think that was God?"

"I don't have any question at all," he said.

"Well, what have you done with it?" I asked.

"My mama didn't raise fools," he said.

So this was not just an idiosyncratic experience of mine.

Later, a long time before my mind was right, I was asked by the Atlanta Integrity Chapter to come and celebrate the Eucharist. They knew that I was an enemy, but they made the invitation: "Would you celebrate the Eucharist and conduct a discussion about the charismatic movement?"

I took the dare and I went. Halfway through the celebration, I felt the Lord speak. And the Lord asked, "How do your cheeks feel?" And I realized they were all cramped from this rictus grin of pseudo-comfort that I was using to show everybody how comfortable I was.

And the Lord said, "Quit that. You don't need to do that. Look around. You're in the kingdom." And I looked around and I was. We had a fantastic discussion afterwards, although one man reserved judgment on the charismatic movement, saying, "Man, I already belong to one despised minority, why should I join a second?"

Following that, the leadership group of that Integrity Chapter formed themselves as a prayer group. And I felt like Jonah, sitting under that wormy leaf, waiting on the city to get burned by God, and realizing God ain't gonna burn 'em, God loves 'em.

God used episodes like that with me to call my attention to the fact, "Gray, it's time you change on this one. I'm not where you are." And so I have changed. And there has been grace in that. It hasn't been pure grace by any extent. Although, I suppose having your character built can be thought of as gracious.

But the grace is a vastly expanded sense of how much God loves me, a vastly expanded sense of how many things in me that I thought reprehensible are precious to God. These experiences have felt to me like spirit, the Holy Spirit, God's Holy Spirit. And something changed in me that's difficult to explain—since moving in that deeper sense of the love of God for me personally, being good is easier. It's as though, when you receive the love of God in more fullness the law of God becomes more natural; it's no longer something external. I covet that for all of us.

A more down-to-earth comparison may be taken from the notion of "kin selection" in evolutionary psychology, which posits that our preference for people like ourselves is hard-wired into our DNA.[1] "Kin selection" has something to do with why we reject people who are crippled, people of different races or languages, people who look different from ourselves. This preference is not a vice that we develop; we are born with it.

And there's evidence that our repugnance to the mannerisms of homosexual people is similarly hard-wired into our DNA. It has to do with the premise that we are in pursuit of children and grandchildren. But the Holy Spirit is there to keep our biology from being our destiny. The Holy Spirit is there to teach us that we can transcend our horror of the other, of the strange.

And every time we do that, it seems to me, the human race spiritually gains yardage.

I constantly have to make this leap with people I disagree with. I constantly have to ask God to show me what's admirable in them, to congratulate God for people I don't agree with. Recently, I was on a board in the diocese talking about these issues. I turned to an erstwhile friend of mine who bitterly disagrees with me on the sexuality issue and I said, "I want you to know that in spite of our disagreement, I know that it's the Jesus-driven pastor's heart in you that doesn't want to weaken the law on this, because you really think this is wrong and it would harm people to give way on this. And I want you to know that I know that's godly and I can see Jesus at work in you."

And, after a pause, he said, "Well, thanks." Later on he asked, "Was there something you wanted me to say?"

I said, "I wish it were possible for you to say—and mean it—that you understood that my pressing my point had something with the love of God as I apprehend it."

He said, "Well Gray, you wouldn't want me to lie about that."

So my task is to discern the grace of God in this dear pastor's heart when in my flesh I cannot, but in my prayers I can. So can you. God gave the church the gift of discernment. We're able to detect the presence or absence of grace in things and people. That's the fastest way I know to let the Spirit of God lift us off the plane of conflict where nothing will ever be resolved to a self-transcendent realm of Christ where we really are like Jesus.

* * *

I want to close with one of my favorite stories—one by Giovanni Guareschi concerning a Catholic priest, Don Camillo, in the Po Valley of Italy following World War II. During the War, Don Camillo had been a chaplain with the anti-Fascist partisan fighters in the mountains. Today, Christmas Eve of 1947, his former comrade/charges were confirmed Stalinists and in political control of the village.

One of the Communists, in an argument with his Catholic wife, had refused to attend the Christmas Eve Mass at which his son was to recite. Soon the quarrel spread all through the village and all the Communist men vowed to boycott the service. Don Camillo went right on planning the gala event with their wives and kids, fully assisted, he thought, by Christ—who often addressed him vocally (when he chose to listen) from the crucifix over the altar.

The service went splendidly, notwithstanding the absence of the obdurate men. Afterwards, mid-evening, Don Camillo stood in front of the crucifix rejoicing at how well the service went. "Didn't you just love how it went, Lord?" he asked.

"I don't know," replied Christ—"I wasn't there." Dumbfounded, Don Camillo asked where he'd been. "I was across the square at the Communist meeting hall where your old friends were gathered miserable."

Without a word, Don Camillo got to his feet. He went to a closet and rummaged around to find an old, battered, olive-green, wooden carton which he tucked under his arm.

He strode out of the rectory, across the square, up to the door of the Communist hall.

"Blam!" went the door as he pounded it open with his massive fist.

"Wham!" went the box as he slammed it down on the table up front, after swiping all the official papers onto the floor.

Right there on the desk, he opened the box and set up the old Communion kit he'd used as their chaplain. He gestured wordlessly to the mayor and various of his henchmen to take their accustomed places as acolytes. They went through the Mass together, missing none of the old familiar responses, all receiving Communion.

When Mass was ended, Don Camillo repacked his carton and lifted it again.

He snorted.

They snorted.

He left the building without a word spoken.

None was needed.

God grant us all the like grace.

Q&A

Question: The one thing that seemed absent from your presentation was the one that the so-called fundamentalists come down on, and that is the *sola scriptura* part of the argument. That is, how do you reconcile your conversion to your point of view with some fairly clear scriptural references?

TEMPLE: My difficulty with fundamentalists is their unwillingness to expose the reading strategies by which they read the Bible to public view. No fundamentalist is a literalist. You can't be a literalist with the Bible. Fundamentalists know that better than we do.

So they have a very elaborate system for the specific weighting of some passages over against others. It would be possible to produce, in theory, a perfectly gracious, outgoing, pacifistic ministry to the poor based on fundamentalist principles. You just need a different reading strategy through the Bible. The difficulty is that *sola scriptura* simply does not work. It simply says it works. But the *sola scriptura* people never acknowledge the application of reason that catalyzes the whole process.

So when someone starts throwing Leviticus at me, I would say, "Could we agree on some hermeneutic principles? Could we compare reading strategies? And could we at least 'fess up to the fact that human reason is an ineluctable part of this process?"

Question: Could you make any comment on tradition and the role tradition has played in interpreting the Scripture over these thousands of years?

TEMPLE: A friend of mine makes the observation that tradition is not wearing your grandmama's hat. Tradition is having a baby. And so one of the criteria I would bring to the discussion is whether we are talking about custom, which tends to be static, or tradition, whether or not it's dynamic, whether or not it lends itself to the evolution of novelty. I think of tradition as yeasty— it produces life.

I think tradition has enormous force, but I think of tradition as process rather than as content. Tradition is always a potentially political act of choice. There are traditionalists in the Episcopal Church who say that women should not be active in different aspects of Christian ministry. They have chosen to overlook, for example, the Beguines in Northern Europe during the Middle Ages, which was a fantastic alternative community in which women were the very point and backbone of the thing. They're overlooking the episcopate of Hilda of Whitby, an influential abbess on the east coast of England, and St. Catherine of Siena, a nun, and an advisor to popes, prelates, and kings.

Question: First of all, I appreciate your emphasis on grace. I think that's been missing a lot. And I feel challenged by your words in terms of that. I'm struggling, though, with the need for balancing of grace with truth. I have friends who've experienced grace in a car accident and they haven't made the car accident into a good thing. I have parishoners I've been struggling with, who find God's grace in reading pornography. I've got folks who get grace from all kinds of relationships that I find to be abusive and yet their experience is that they are graceful. So at some point the grace has to be balanced with truth.

TEMPLE: It's terribly important that, in the question of whether something is gracious, we bring the gift of discernment to bear on it. The paradigm for this, that I think maybe Louie will touch on, is St. Peter's conversion on the roof of Simon the tanner where tradition, as he understood it in the Scripture, was against him. The only thing going for him was that fact that he'd walked the three years with Jesus and had some sense of Jesus' style.

So what I would urge, even with the guy who says that pornography is a grace in his life, is that you discern what is going on spiritually in that exchange. Now I have a hunch how that one's going to come out. But there are some others that I think would be more ambiguous.

So I would throw it back on discernment as heavily as on any written code. Again, you could have predicted that answer, because I'm liberal and that's how we do it.

Question: You talked about seeing the grace in others whom you may disagree with, and while in your flesh you may wish that was different, in your spirit you would pray with them, be with them, and honor them. That's difficult sometimes. How do you get through that tension when it's probably true that the expression by some of conservative views contributes to social or political climates where people lose jobs, don't get jobs, get beat up, and get murdered? How do we live in that?

TEMPLE: I've been known to scold. Two weeks ago I made exactly that point with a very dear friend of mine who is quite conservative. I said to her, "You're contributing to a climate that hurts people, and you're not a harmful person. Examine what you're doing." It took us two days, but we're friends again. And, while she didn't say that she conceded the point, I think she caught it to some extent.

The other thing that I try to do is to joke a great deal. And I joke very seriously. I think that was one of our Lord's chief characteristics. It was so obvious, that nobody says anything about it. But it ought to be clear to us how frequently he has a twinkle in his eye.

We know scientifically that our reptilian complexes, limbic systems and the neocortices are not linked together very well.[2] The two human functions that we know link those three layers of our brains are tears and laughter. And so I think it's a mitzvah. I think it's a sacred duty that we attempt to go into any Christian activity light-heartedly, merrily looking for the merriment of the Savior.

CHAPTER 2

THE GREAT APOLOGETIC TASK
Reaffirming and Renewing Marriage

by DIANE KNIPPERS

Diane LeMasters Knippers is the President of the Institute on Religion and Democracy (IRD) in Washington, DC, founded in 1981 by clergy and laity who seek spiritual and political reform within their churches. Mrs. Knippers directs the Episcopal Action program of the IRD, which seeks to reform the public witness of the Episcopal Church. She also directs the IRD's Ecumenical Coalition on Women and Society, composed of Protestant, Catholic and Orthodox women. The purpose of the Coalition is to counter forms of radical feminism in church and society.

In 1995, Mrs. Knippers led a team of women to the United Nations Fourth World Conference on Women in Beijing, China, where she successfully lobbied for the inclusion of an affirmation of the right of religious freedom in the Platform for Action. She has recently traveled to Turkey and met with Christians there.

She has had personal contact with persecuted Christians from Iran, Egypt, Nigeria, and elsewhere. She speaks widely on the subject of the persecuted church to church and civic groups and on radio shows.

I understand that not too long ago my rector, Martin Minns, was having a telephone conversation with Bishop Lee about some issues facing the church. And at one point Bishop Lee interrupted the conversation and said something along the lines of, "Time's up. I only talk about sex one hour a day."

Now, if this is really Bishop Lee's personal rule, I'm entirely sympathetic. And I'm sorry we're all breaking this rule for these two days. There is a danger with all this sex talk. We can kill the mystery with too much dissection. We can debase our society by treating intimate matters too cavalierly.

Then there's the problem of how to talk about sex. Do I take the clinical route and discuss penile-vaginal intercourse versus anal intercourse or oral sex? Won't that disgust some and challenge my own sense of propriety, especially standing before a mixed group—a church group no less?

The traditional terms such as sodomy offend others, because they imply a moral judgment. So most of us end up using euphemisms like "same-sex" partners, which may be more tasteful, but lack precision to the point of dishonesty. After all, it's not "partners"—as in business or ballroom-dancing—that cause the controversy. You don't have to be a prude to worry about losing our proper respect for God's good gift of sex by talking about it immodestly or dishonestly.

So it is with real trepidation that I proceed. Despite the risks, the current debates offer a great opportunity for the gospel. The opportunity is to rediscover and reaffirm God's plan for human sexuality, for marriage and the family. It is an opportunity to explore this great mystery, rooted in creation itself, reflected in our physical nature, and in every society in human history. It is an opportunity to renew marriage as it reflects the very image of the relationship between God and his people.

Our parents and our grandparents took these things for granted. We and our children cannot. So the gospel opportunity is for our generation also a great apologetic task. It forces us to ask basic questions of humanity. What is a human person? What is the relation of body and person? How were we created and why? How is human society to be organized and to what purpose? Why is there sin and evil? Why is there suffering? And what is the measure of God's mercy and grace?

I intend to do three things in this paper. First, I want to share with you my deepest convictions about our nature as sexual beings, about marriage, and about family. Secondly, I want to discuss my deep concern about the disintegration of contemporary family life. And finally, I will outline what I believe is the task before the church—a task that begins with, but moves far beyond, compellingly reasserting its historic teaching—that genital sexual behavior should be reserved for life-long, faithful marriage between a man and a woman.

I said I would share my deepest convictions, but I want to make clear that I don't think these are merely my own ideas or preferences or even my own experiences. I have tried to be faithful to the plain teaching of the whole biblical witness and to the Judeo-Christian tradition—that is to the witness and teachings of the people of God for millennia. Furthermore, as one with a background in sociology, I have tried to construct a reasoned view of what is needed at this moment in our social history. In other words, I am bold to offer my convictions, shaped and determined by Scripture, tradition, and reason, as a witness to God's truth. So I ask not for you to affirm my experiences, but to test whether my assertions are true to what God has revealed.

If God in Christ calls us to a certain moral standard, then we must strive to obey—even if it is not comfortable or congruent with our lives, even if we don't understand why. But I'm here to say that traditional biblical teaching does make sense.

What is that teaching that I would defend? I believe it was concisely and accurately rendered in a resolution adopted at our 1994 Diocesan Council here in Virginia, quoting Bishop Lee when it reaffirmed, "The diocese is consistently faithful to the church's teaching that the normative context for sexual intimacy is life-long, heterosexual, monogamous marriage. . . ."

Human sexuality is rooted in our physical nature as created beings. We are two sexes, fearfully and wonderfully made for each other. A man's body was created to enable him to enter a woman, to fit into her, and her body was created to receive him and his seed. The man and the woman were created to desire one another and to give one another pleasure. A woman's body—so we are reminded every month—was created to nurture new life, to provide life-giving sustenance and care, both before and after a child is born. Physically, intellectually, emotionally, spiritually, a man and a woman are given what they need to nurture and sustain the infant human being through childhood and until that son or daughter is in turn ready to fulfill his or her own calling.

This is the great and wonderful mystery of God's creation. My friends Jay and Catherine have a brand new baby. I remember meeting little Emma in the undercroft, after her Baptism one Sunday afternoon this fall. I admired her little face and hands—and we marveled over the miracle of those ten perfectly formed tiny fingers.

Our sexuality is such a miracle and source of wonder. We must treat it with a reverent awe as a gift of God.

But we are more than physical creatures. We are also created as social creatures. God's plan for humankind is that its primary and most basic organization is in families. Interestingly, this is affirmed in the United Nations Universal Declaration of Human Rights, which asserts that the family is the fundamental unit of society.

Families start with a marriage. That's why we understand that marriage is not merely a private contractual relationship.

Marriage is a social institution, and society, because it has a stake in marriage, has a stake in its definition. Therefore, we do not allow someone to marry close blood relatives, legally incompetent persons, minors, members of the same sex, or multiple partners. None of these limitations would be valid if marriage were simply a private arrangement expressing mutual love, comfort and commitment.

There are various goods to marriage—unity, procreation, mutual joy, help and comfort, sexual discipline, social cohesion and, perhaps most awesomely, to exemplify the covenantal relationship between God and his people. This latter is one of the great themes of Scripture, developed from Genesis to Hosea, through the New Testament to Revelation. Martin Luther said, "Faith. . .unites the soul with Christ, as a bride is united with her bridegroom. From such a marriage, as St. Paul says [Ephesians 5:31-33], it follows that Christ and the soul become one body, so that they hold all things in common.

My husband and I take seriously this calling—to live out in our marriage an image of the faithful, long-suffering, sacrificial, joyful commitment of God to his people. This is marriage's evangelistic purpose, if you will. Thus, good marriages proclaim the gospel—the good news that can transform lives and nations.

As I said, there are several purposes for marriage, some of which may be fulfilled in other human institutions as well. Ironically, the ones that seem to get the most emphasis—mutual joy, help and comfort—are the least particular to marriage. There are and should be many other relationships besides marriage in which we walk with one another through life's challenges.

So I want to highlight two purposes which are unique to marriage and which make marriage constitutive of human society. I will discuss the unitive and pro-creative goods of marriage.

The unitive function is classically described in Scripture—the two shall become one flesh. It is not good for man to be alone. "One flesh" is a radical critique of the autonomous individualism so rampant in our society. It is a union so intimate and so complete that we may be said to belong to one another. My husband has rights to me and my body—and I have rights to him and to his body.

But this unitive function doesn't merely unite two individuals. There is a great difference and divide in the human family—the two sexes. In marriage, we are united with "the other." In marriage we are pushed out of the comfort zone of our own gender. We are now together with a very different type of person. On a personal level, the challenges of this relationship can produce maturity and growth. But socially in uniting with the other sex, we unite the two halves of the human family, preventing a kind of sexual apartheid, similar to that which humankind has already proved itself so capable.

The procreative function is also expressed in Scripture—"Be fruitful and multiply." Marriage is intended as a means of bringing other human beings into existence—to perpetuate the human race. We are given the extraordinary privilege of being co-creators with God.

In recent decades, the procreative function of sexuality and marriage has been increasingly marginalized. Birth control and abortion technology, increased acceptance of extra-marital sexual pleasure as an end in itself, and a social order less and less child-friendly—these are trends that have contributed to the delinking of sexual intercourse and childbearing. And I wonder whether this has all been to the good.

Now, I hasten to add that I am not suggesting that we all accept Catholic doctrine. But I am suggesting that even we Episcopalians would do well to re-examine the unintended consequences of these social trends. We must rediscover a link between love, expressed in the intimate self-giving and sexual intercourse, and, growing out of that love, an openness to the creation of human life.

The unitive and procreative goods of marriage are fulfilled in many ways. But they are preeminently fulfilled in what is what is called "the marriage act"—sexual intercourse. Indeed this "marriage act" is necessary to what we call the consummation of marriage. A marriage is consummated, not by the mutual vows, or the proclamation of a priest, or by having children—it is consummated by sexual intercourse.

My brother has a bumper sticker that reads, "Practice Safe Sex. Get Married and Be Faithful." Of course, the word SEX is in BIG letters and I'm sure he's going to have an accident some day, if people try to read his bumper sticker as he's driving down the road. But I've been thinking about this. Is marriage "safe sex"? Well, physically, of course it is, much safer than other kinds. But I call it "high risk" sex as well. Some call it heroic enterprise. In marriage, you give yourself completely to another. You give your body—husband and wife possess one another. And we take incredible risks of pain, hurt and loss from spouse or child. So, yes, marrying and raising a family can yield safety and security and fulfillment and joy, but it is also one of the most difficult, challenging and even terrifying things one will ever do. Brides and grooms are right to be nervous on their wedding day.

Let me say a quick, but necessary word regarding single and childless persons. God intends, and optimal human life requires, that every human person have a family—that is, to be born into a family. But God does not intend for every person to marry. Some are called to celibate singleness. A necessary corollary is this: Genital sexual expression is not a prerequisite for full humanity.

Moreover, some couples are incapable of having children. My husband and I are among those who experience this disappointment.

There is simply not time to discuss all of the issues around singleness and childlessness adequately. Suffice it to say that men and women who do not marry or have children are entirely capable of living out God's great and good plan for their lives. But all of us, in whatever marital state, have a responsibility to work to preserve, strengthen and sustain the necessary, but fragile, institutions of marriage and family.

So what? What does this classic view of marriage and sexuality have to do with the practice of homosexuality? Let me respond to those who are working very hard to legitimize homosexual practice, within society and especially within the church.

First, there are those whose unabashed agenda is to change the institution of marriage. Second, there are those who want to include homosexuals in the institution of marriage. This would, either intentionally or unintentionally, change marriage by definition and by practice. Finally, there are those who advocate only same-sex "unions," and who want to keep heterosexual marriage as it is. This would, I will argue, finally have the unintended consequence of changing marriage as well.

First, let's look at those who want to change the institution of marriage. Participants at the April 1997 "Beyond Inclusion Conference" at All Saints Episcopal Church in Pasadena criticized marriage as sexist, patriarchal, hetrosexist and violent. One participant observed, "I've started to think that maybe we are a threat to marriage as we know it, and maybe the church needs to redefine marriage." An Episcopal priest agreed, "It [gay union] does threaten the primacy of heterosexual marriage, which is based on sexism." Another priest admitted that the church's blurring the boundaries of marriage would affect the large society. But he went on to say, "Deconstructing these categories . . . is a part of the gospel work."[3]

Indeed, a consultation of Episcopalians has prepared draft rites to bless same-sex unions. The rites could be used for both heterosexual and homosexual couples and they include no pledges of life-long monogamous faithfulness. Put quite simply, there are persons in the church who consider the idea of life-long fidelity in either homosexual or heterosexual relationships, not only hopelessly outdated, but repressive. These persons want to use homosexual unions intentionally to break down and redefine marriage. They call this justice. I call it unjust—an attack on the common good. Marriages deliberately designed not to be permanent and exclusive undermine the very purposes for which God gave us marriage. They fall far short of joining two persons in one inseparable flesh. They do not provide an apt environment for the procreation of children. And they certainly do not bear adequate witness to the unbreakable jealous love of God for his people.

But what of those who simply want to broaden marriage to include same-sex couples, or merely to offer same-sex couples a marriage-like set of benefits and acknowledgments, while not calling those relationships marriage? These folks look at the narcissistic, hedonistic, promiscuous nature of some of the homosexual sub-culture and they want to help. They make the argument that if the church blesses same-sex marriages, or same-sex unions, it will have the effect of providing stable, healthy relationships. This is a very appealing and well intentioned argument.

Of course, one answer to this is that God in Scripture teaches that sexual liaisons between persons of the same sex are wrong and the church cannot bless what God declares sin. I believe that's a very good answer indeed. But, I am also convinced that their well intentioned plan would not work and would have other destructive consequences.

Logically, I believe, once you allow same-sex unions or marriages, you have undercut any moral argument to other limits on the practice of human sexuality. On what basis do you argue for monogamy at all? How do you respond to the person who says, "Call off your old tired ethics. If I want to enjoy a sexual relationship with one person, or two, or twelve a night, it's no concern of yours"? How do you answer the person who says, "I'm bisexual and I was born that way. Don't limit me to just one sexual partner "? What do we say to consenting adults who practice sado-masochism? Could we continue to make polygamy or polyandry illegal? What about those in England who want to lower the age of consent for homosexuals to 16, in effect legalizing what we still call pederasty?

I'm not being provocative; I'm being sincere. I don't know how we could or would, as a church, say no to these real sexual trends after we have embraced homosexuality. Once we have cast off God's gold standard of marriage, how will we ever invent or agree upon and enforce a substitute standard? The only substitutes that I've heard proposed are vague notions such as that persons should have sex only with mutual consent and love between them. But we all know many persons in objectively damaging relationships who can offer the excuse, "But we love one another." That is not enough of a standard. And God has given us a higher standard. Finally, I find the position of those who want to bless same sex "unions," but not call it marriage, incredibly naive. You cannot sustain that distinction for a moment. In the church, you have leaders such as Bishop Spong lambasting this view as prejudicial and equating it to a defense of slavery or apartheid. And outside the church, you have a court in Hawaii on the verge of requiring same-sex marriage under that state's Equal Rights Amendment. If the church accepts same-sex unions as was proposed at last summer's General Convention, it is only ivory-towered theologians capable of endlessly debating theological minutia who will be able to discern the difference between marriage and union.

There is one more reason same-sex marriage wouldn't work as a stabilizing influence. There is no evidence that more than a few homosexual couples would really take advantage of it. Of course, a poll might show a majority of homosexuals asking the church to offer such a rite. But what they want is legitimization—for the larger culture and especially the church to say, "You are okay and what you do sexually is okay." This we cannot and must not do. It validates behavior that would further undermine marriage and the family.

Now, to help you understand the real urgency that I feel about these matters, let me turn to the state of the family in American society. We live in a society that is abandoning the view of marriage and sexuality that I've outlined. For over 40 years, we have systematically forsaken biblical standards for sexual behavior and so we have deconstructed the family. And as a result, we live in a society that is experiencing social devastation, particularly among the poorest and the most vulnerable populations.

My generation fomented what we called the sexual revolution. Our children and our children's children are the combat casualties, the victims, of this revolution. When so many boasted of having sex while holding back from the one-flesh union of marriage, when so many tried to deny or evade the obvious connection between the marriage act and child-bearing, we taught our children lessons about love that we never intended. We taught them that human love—and perhaps God's love—may be no more than a passing emotion, without full investment of self, without sacrifice, without staying power. And too many of our children are living out this grievous lesson that we taught them.

So what is the state of the American family at this moment? It is a social institution in deep trouble. "For the average American, the probability that a marriage taking place today will end in divorce or permanent separation is calculated to be a staggering 60 percent."[4] In 1960, five percent of all live births were out-of-wedlock. In 1970, it was 10 percent. In 1997, 33 percent. Four out of 10 children will go to bed tonight in a home in which their father does not reside.[5] In the District of Columbia, eight out of ten African-American children live without their father.

Contrary to conventional wisdom, social pathologies affecting children correlate more closely to family disintegration than to factors such as poverty and ethnicity. What is the status of child well-being? Juvenile violent crime has increased six-fold from 1960 to 1995. Reports of child neglect and abuse have quintupled since 1976. Eating disorders and rates of unipolar depression have soared among adolescent girls. Teen suicide has tripled. Alcohol and drug abuse rates may have leveled off, but they continue at high rates.[6]

Let me be clear, I do not blame homosexuals for this degeneration of marriage and the family. But isn't it obvious that the campaign to win greater legitimacy for homosexual behavior is a logical extension of the sexual revolution? Isn't it a part of a larger cultural idolatry of sexual gratification?

Even if I did not consider sexual gratification between two men or two women immoral, I would oppose the campaign to legitimize it as imprudent and dangerous at this social moment. It sends all the wrong messages to the heterosexual majority who already find it so easy to be irresponsible. It tells them that the church is prepared to help them justify any sexual relationship in which they perceive some kind of commitment—even if that commitment falls far short of what God intended in marriage or what is required for social stability.

Many social institutions—governmental and in civil society—must play a role in restoring and rebuilding the family. An urgent task for the church is to rediscover Christian teaching about sexuality. We live, as I said, in a society that hammers away against this view of sexuality and marriage in every way possible. If the church does not teach celibacy in singleness and fidelity in life-long marriage between a man and a woman, who will? But our further task is to develop the ministries necessary to help people live by that standard, as well as ministries to those whose lives have been broken by failures.

We live in a society that has made sex an idol. In her book, *By Sexual Character*, Marva Dawn, borrowing some of the social insights of Ellul, writes that this idolatry is made more severe by the lack of intimacy in our technological milieu, and the desperation of people to fill that void.

The stakes are enormous, not just for the church, but for our society—for the common good. In order to serve the common good—and in order to be true to its own purposes and truths—the church must be counter-cultural.

But what does that require? It requires that the body of Christ exhibit the attributes of God—holiness, justice, love, truth, grace and compassion. Let me make some observations on how these attributes will be embodied.

Holiness. We worship a Holy God who demands that each of us live holy lives. The church sustains us in that quest, first by teaching what is required to live a holy life sexually. But we must do more than teach; we must equip and support. Programs aimed at young people, such as the True Love Waits program, should be developed in every congregation.

The church must also recognize the importance of healthy gender development in living a holy life. Ironically, at the United Nations Beijing Women's Conference, it was the most liberal feminists who said that gender was a social construct. (In fact, some of us wore buttons that said, "Sex is Better Than Gender." The buttons represented our playful attempt to say that biological design mattered too.) Yet, in the debates regarding homosexuality, the more liberal position is that one's sexuality is a given, immutable and not amenable to social factors. Many people even make the preposterous claim that there's the scientific support for such rigid determinism.

Frankly, scientific study about the development of sexual preference and gender identity is in its infancy. But some of the best medical and psychological study is consistent with what most of us know by common sense and experience: that gender identity and sexual desire is a complex product of both nature and nurture.

Thus, it is crucial that we nurture healthy and whole gender development in our children. This is why we must pay much more attention to the importance of fathers in particular, and healthy male and female role models in general. Because healthy and normal gender development matters, because role models matter, because sexual habits formed at an early age matter—then it also matters that our schools and churches teach that homosexual behavior is not morally equivalent to heterosexual marriage.

In other words, while we adults indulge our moral confusions in our dialogues and Burning Issues Conferences, it is the next generation that will pay a very serious price. While we are unable to tell our teenagers what is right and what is wrong—and while we are unable to tell them by what moral authority we make those judgments—they are exploring and testing their options and many are engaging in destructive experiments and making deadly choices. Holiness is possible in our day. Healthy gender development will help foster such holiness.

Justice. The just ordering of society, requires the preservation of the family. No other institution in society can do what our religious institutions can do to preserve marriages. And it can start with programs such as pre-marital counseling, marriage encounters, mentoring programs and the like. With compassion and conviction, we must work to discourage divorce and out-of-wedlock births.

Love. The church must make a radical stand against rampant individualism and for community. This requires sacrifice for the common good, sometimes of one's own personal desires. But it also requires a commitment to hospitality and friendship. People are desperately lonely in our transient and technological society. Persons with a homosexual orientation and many single and married heterosexuals are lonely. Some turn to sexual intimacy simply to fill the gaping loneliness. That is a failure of friendship, a failure of community. And a failure of our church.

Truth. The church must tell the truth. Very few people want to talk about the physical damage wrought by much homosexual activity. Studies show that the average homosexual man has a life expectancy decades shorter than heterosexual men do. It is not just HIV-AIDS or other sexually transmitted diseases related to promiscuity. It is also higher rates of cancer and other disorders, related to practices such as anal intercourse. The human body is abused when it is put to uses for which it was not designed. This is just one of the life-sustaining truths the church needs to tell.

Compassion. The compassionate church needs to be able to answer this question: "How can it be faithful or loving to deny homosexuals sexual pleasure?" On one level the question reveals the sexual idolatry of our day—that it is unthinkably unjust to deny sexual pleasure to anyone. But the truth is that some homosexuals may never be able to live normal heterosexual lives. They are like the alcoholic who can never go into a bar. The fact is that we are calling homosexuals to a life of self-denial. Obedience to God can mean a life of struggle and sacrifice. Saying that you can legitimately enjoy homosexual relations and avoid the suffering of self-denial is the prosperity gospel of the Left. We must recognize that suffering—suffering for Christ's sake—is not so unusual in this world. That is the witness of Job, of Bonnhoeffer, and of countless believers imprisoned for their faith today.

But the church offers more than this difficult, albeit sometimes ennobling, truth. There is the ministry of compassion. After we've done what we can to alleviate suffering or to ameliorate it through friendship and community, we can hold them and weep with them. We can point them to the One who suffered the ultimate denial and death for our sakes.

Finally, there is grace. The church must proclaim and offer the grace of God. Grace that forgives every sin. This is the good news for each person in this room. God's grace is available to every sinner—from the man who engages in anal intercourse with his male companion to the more prevalent forms of heterosexual sin—adultery, fornication, pornography, and fantasy from hardcore to Harlequin. This grace does even more than forgive. God's grace does change lives.

* * *

I want to conclude by telling you about a friend of mine whose life has been changed. Shirley Black would have been here today, but she's in Haiti working on a development project to aid that beleaguered nation.

Shirley has experienced and joined in some tragic abuses of sexuality, but now she has found God's grace. As a child, she was abandoned by her father and abused by her stepfather. She was hurt and disappointed in relationships with men. Then Shirley was drawn into a lesbian relationship that was followed by a series of relationships for many years.

Her testimony is riveting. Through a series of events some seven years ago, she heard God calling her to leave those unhealthy relationships. God led her to a caring woman who discipled and supported her in her process of transformation that took over two years. Shirley joined a home group that knew her and supported her. She went through the Living Waters course. She experienced deep healing prayer. She was sustained by a community of faith that loved her, invited her into their homes, prayed with her and wept with her. It was costly and difficult for Shirley and her friends. But this compassionate community was a means of God's grace in Shirley's life.

Last week I had breakfast with Shirley to get her advice. "What should the church do," I asked, "to help men and women who are facing homosexual temptation?"

She told me two things. "First, the church must tell the truth. Don't send an ambiguous message. I knew it was wrong. Don't compromise." Secondly, Shirley said, "The church must be ready to welcome those struggling with their sexuality. We must welcome them in our homes and in our sanctuaries. We must commit to costly, loving, caring discipleship." Shirley is now a counselor for other women. But she gets many more calls for help than she can take on. Tears filled her eyes and she implored me, "We must reach out and share the love and transforming power of Christ."

Shirley's testimony and her challenge are why I am convinced we have before us—not a gospel threat—but a gospel opportunity. It only awaits our confident and loving embrace.

Q&A

Question: I want to briefly make a statement about myself. I am a 54-year-old man and did not recognize my homosexuality until I was 43 years old. I was conscious of the fact that I was a homosexual from the time I was a young child. I grew up in a culture and a church and a family which did not approve of homosexuality. I grew up believing that I was immoral and heathen. But it was present very early in my life and I repressed it. That, and a lot of other things that happened to me as a young man in a very violent South, caused me to stop talking to God. I denied my sexuality. I spent 43 years as a straight man.

Things eventually got so bad for me that I was catatonic. They found me in the corner of my bedroom in Charlottesville and had to carry me into the crisis intervention center of the University of Virginia Medical Center. It took a month before I could talk and it took several years to rebuild certain facets of my childhood.

According to the definition in your paper, I came into this church with a not very healthy gender identity. But I tried. I want you to know that. I tried! And I respect what you're saying tonight, but I truly cannot believe that I, as a gay man, I am some bizarre social artifice that will die ten years earlier than my brothers that surround me here tonight.

I am a child of God. I am Episcopalian. I have found peace and comfort and love and respect in this church, and I have found a role in it. I have tried, as have my gay brothers and sisters, whether they speak up or sit silent tonight, to contribute in this church. And that's not merely because I'm afraid that nobody's going to love me. That's because I realized a number of years ago, that God truly loves me and I truly love God. And if I love God, the way to express that, gracefully, is by loving my brothers and sisters and acting kindly toward them.

KNIPPERS: I want to be sure that I've clearly expressed my point of view. I do not for one moment question that you are a child of God or that he loves you. And if I've communicated erroneously in that regard, I just want to clarify it. Thank you for sharing and the courage that it took.

CHAPTER 3

TRADITIONS IN CONFLICT

by JAMES STANTON

James Stanton was born in 1946 in Kansas, and grew up in Southern California. He graduated from the Southern California School of Theology with the degree of Doctor of Ministry, in 1975, and was ordained in the Christian Church (Disciples of Christ). He was ordained a deacon in the Diocese of Los Angeles, and a priest in the Diocese of San Joaquin in 1977. He served congregations in San Joaquin and Iowa. In 1992, while serving as Rector of St. Mark's Church in Glendale, California, he was elected the sixth Bishop of Dallas. He was consecrated on March 6, 1993. Married in 1968 to Diane Hanson, he is the father of Jennifer and Justin.

I want to begin by saying that I, like Gray Temple, do not like the confrontational aspect of this business. I don't think we make any progress in legislative bodies, for example. I don't find it very useful to try to sum up things of great moment in three-minute segments in debate at General Convention. Thirty minutes is not much better, but it is better. What I want to do in this time is try to sketch out a basic position and then have as much give and take as we can.

There are a number of things said so far that I have agreed with, and some I have disagreed with. I partly agree with Gray Temple when he says conflicts are unresolvable at the level they are waged. And I think his example of Bosnia is an interesting one because the conflict in Bosnia hasn't been resolved—it's a war. The character of a war is to get the upper hand and impose a resolution. I suspect the real conflict there will never be resolved until it gets in the form of argument, where there's a discussion, where folks deal with words and perceptions. Therefore, I don't take quite so a dim a view of the presentation of arguments.

When Diane Knippers states that we don't want to accept catholic doctrine, what do the words mean, what are the patterns into which they fall? It all hangs on the word, for example, "tradition." We have said that we are a catholic church, and that has some consequences, unless the word "catholic" is merely a form with no substance and the idea of "tradition" is simply empty or vague. With her, I want to say that this "tradition" has a substantial and discernible content.

When Gray Temple warned against front-loading arguments, he used the example of Hegelianism. There's no way we can avoid front-loading the issue. And I want to show you why. It's not just the Hegelian problem, which I would regard as something mechanical. It is something fundamental, something absolutely key to the impasse in which we find ourselves in the church today.

All our words gain their meaning from the tradition in which they are located.

What we are facing today is a conflict of traditions. We tend to look at the word tradition and think in terms of the past, the way something has come to us with all its changes and permutations. What I want us to do is conceptualize it in a slightly different way. That is, what we are seeing in this debate is a conflict of traditions in which the very words we use are already rooted in a certain kind of understanding. And what actually is being proposed, it seems to me, is the supplanting of one tradition by the other so that, while the same words can be used, they mean very different things.

Traditions provide a structure in which words mean something. And one way to get at structure is story. I always ask, "What is the story that is being told here?" Another way to approach this subject is to ask, "What purpose does a human being serve?" You can answer that question in terms of story and see what the purpose of being human is. What is the purpose of life? What is the purpose of your life?

There are different kinds of things being said here. The story last night—told in response to Diane Knippers's presentation—was very compelling. We tend to find stories compelling. But I want to ask, what is the structure of the story that is being told? How does it answer questions such as, What is the purpose of life? What am I for? What is somebody else for? What's God for in this whole picture? Because this is the way we get at ultimate questions.

Carter Heyward writes, "We yearn for mutuality. . . . We live in these tensions of affirmation and lamentation. What we want most terrifies us most—passionate connectedness with one another that will draw us sharply into our identities as persons in relation to our work and in our love. Our way to God, through the moral clutter of alienation [I would take that phrase to mean, the way traditional moral ethics has caused us to be alienated from ourselves], is with one another's solidarity, in faith that none of us is alone. Our sacred power, the erotic, pulls us toward this embodied realization."[7] What are we here for? For developing our identities through relationship. Heyward coins the term "godding" for this movement in solidarity with others. We touch God, we indeed create God, in the power of the erotic, the power of the sexual life, and in this way we come to realize who we are. By getting such relationships right, we are furthermore "saved."

Another example: One of the stories in *A Book of Revelations*, published by Integrity, says in part, "For reasons unknowable to me, the capacity to love, which in most people links to sexual desire for persons of the opposite sex, linked me to desire for persons of my same sex. But the love is the same, the desire is the same, and I believe is the same gift of God. As once the church had come to realize that the food that had once been called unclean could now be called clean, that Gentiles who had once been called unclean could now share a meal with Jews who had spent their lives keeping the law, so I have hope that in our time, the embrace of the church will widen once again."[8] What's a person here for? To love. And it is God's work to bring about this capacity to love and be through love. The object of love is not as important as the fact of loving.

Christian language comes very naturally to be used in these stories. God made us. God made us for love. And we become whole *through* love. But there's also a problem. If we compare these stories to the Christian story, the biblical story, we see that it is completely different. God made you, all right, but there's a problem right in the heart of your being. It's something you share with all others. From the very beginning, so to speak, we are built for a certain kind of relationship to God and to one another. But we have tried to bend that God-given purpose and use that gift of life for our own. Is this not told in the story of the garden in Genesis—that we have been, as it were, seduced into something else, turned from a relationship of obedience and adoration and service of God, and *toward* the affirmation of the autonomous self.

This is not merely a problem, it's a disaster. Because this very movement toward the self—affirming the self, or being affirmed by the self, or seeing God as primarily concerned with our selves—breaks all the possibilities of our ever realizing what

God intended for us to be and to become. In fact, the problem here is precisely this business of the self, it's the story of the self.

We can come at the self-story in a number of different ways. I've been listening to these different approaches to filling out this story. We can talk about this self in terms of scientific categories, for example, and we do that a lot. Gray was talking about evolutionary theory, the evolving self or evolving conceptions of the self. Others speak as if the self is somehow defined by the genes or other biochemical processes.

We begin to fill out the picture of this autonomous self. We may describe it in terms of science, as I have said. Or we can go to philosophy, to literature. We begin to use metaphors that we draw from the world, searching for basic first principles to try to figure out what it is the self should do and be.

What fascinates me is the patterns we find when we look at these ways of understanding the self.

Christians always start with God—the self is God's gift. But then, the patterns diverge.

For many, we are alienated from the self. This is the central problem. The solution then seems to be that we ought to affirm ourselves because it is our right to do so. We must come to acceptance of who we are, to self-affirmation. Then we start looking for ways to qualify what affirming the self entails—caring, integrity, honesty, mutuality, and so on.

Some say we can even construct ourselves—define who we are and want to be. This is called courage—the courage to be.

Salvation—healing, wholeness, meaning and direction—seems to be brought about when we find who we are and, as it were, take charge of who we are through self-actualization. This need not—indeed, most often is not—done alone. We come to self-knowing and fulfilment through relationships, especially sexual relationships.

Now, my question is, is this the biblical pattern?

I suggest to you that it is not. The story in Scripture is that by pursuing the self, sin entered into the world and became the problem that has to be dealt with. Therefore, one does not find

God coming to us to affirm the self. Rather, the self is out of communion with God and has no way of restoring itself to communion with God. Sin is a broken relationship. Sin is missing the mark.

What does it mean to miss the mark? In Scripture, missing the mark is something very specific. It is missing what God commands, doing other than what God purposes.

In answer to the question, "What is a person for?" the Bible says the end of human life is to live in a specific kind of obligatory relationship with God. But in pursuing the self, we've broken that relationship—we are sinners—and we can't make it back on our own.

It is very important is to understand the role of sinner and sin in these two pictures. In one, to be a sinner is to do wrong things. I'm a sinner because I've done something wrong. If somehow I can fix up these wrong things, say by living in a more just or mutual way, then I will no longer be a sinner.

But the Christian understanding, as I see it in this tradition, is quite the opposite. You *are* a sinner, implicated in the sin of your race. That is, you are caught up in the pursuit of the self. Therefore, because you are a sinner, you do bad things.

The basic understanding of sinner and sin is that the self is out of sync with God to begin with, and the only way to get back on the right track is to give the self up, to surrender all claim to it, to yield the self to the doing of God's will. Thus the call to repentance. And whether you look at the Old Testament or the New Testament, the pattern is the same. If you look at prophetic religion, the pattern is the same. If you look at law or grace, the pattern is the same.

You are not going to find yourself by going inside, affirming, being affirmed, and building relationships. You find yourself only as you give, only as you yield, only as you surrender in trusting obedience to God. This, as I say, does not fall back on just a few texts, this is a pattern, I think, that is detectable in all of the biblical passages. It's distinguishable as the prophetic tradition. The prophets do not come to announce the new, they come to announce God's direct word and call the people back to the observance of the law. Why? Because the law is God's act of grace, because without knowing God's will and purpose we can't possibly serve it, much less surrender to it. God's revealed word is not the source of the "moral clutter of alienation" some take it to be—it is the only clear way to wholeness possible for us.

In the area of our sexuality, I think this has some very clear implications. We are not what our orientation makes us. We are beings called to bear the image of God. God did not make us homosexual or straight. God made us to do his will on earth as it is in heaven. We do not come to wholeness or communion with God through our own self-affirmation. We get there only in surrendering our selves and letting God remake us from within.

It's not as if by suddenly changing our minds, we can serve God's will. We've got to surrender and then, by God's action we're equipped to do that service. This is the same pattern we find in the life of Jesus.

This tradition is present even in our liturgy. What does it mean, for example, when I go out and confirm people and ask them, "Do you promise to continue in the apostles' teaching and fellowship?" Does that not assume that there is an identifiable thing to commit oneself to? If the apostles' teaching is simply how I construe it, or how my group construes it, or how we sort of make sense of it in terms of modern thought categories, then what am I asking people to commit themselves to? What am I asking them to pledge themselves to?

I don't think we have a right to ask people to make solemn commitments such as that if we really do not believe that there is such an identifiable thing. And yet, to continue in the apostles' teaching and fellowship means to preserve that tradition and its original pattern.

The great sexuality debate is not about sex, it is about the self, what it is for, and wherein lies its salvation, its wholeness, its healing.

Q&A

Question: This concept of the autonomous self being the wrong self and the disobedience in Genesis being the sin, is very much an interpretation by Augustine that was picked up by Calvin and Luther. The earlier tradition actually spoke of Christ as liberating us to be free, to be out of the bondage of sin and so it's quite a different tradition.

In the Jewish tradition, the evil inclination is part of God's good creation, part of the same energy that enables us to gather resources, part of the same energy that is the good energy behind sexuality. That energy can be distorted, and the Jewish tradition would agree with that, but that evil inclination remains part of the good creation of God and not part of some separate evil.

STANTON: Let's take out the autonomous self. Let's talk about whatever kind of self you want, but the direction is the same, the affirmation of the individual in his or her individual identity. That is what is meant by missing the mark. To miss the mark is to miss God's mark. Certainly, if there's any goodness in turning to meet *my* criteria, *my* judgment, *my* agenda, then there can't be any such thing as missing the mark.

Augustine is accurately, adequately, and authentically replicating exactly the same pattern that is found in the Old Testament, that is found in the New Testament. But the real *telos* is the thing that gets disconnected from us. In the Israelite tradition, and all ancient traditions, human beings live in a specific given, a specific kind of relationship. The *telos*, what human beings are for, is answered quite clearly—they are for worshiping God, living in obedience to God, living in a very specific kind of relationship to God. Where the autonomous self emerges is when that telos is taken away; we begin to look at the individual in terms of a self-determining person, making free choices and enacting themselves.

Now the problem with that is that if we say, "Well, I'm a free person, what ought I to do?" we disconnect from the story that gives the question any meaning, particularly for Christians. What are we left with? We go to science and we find criteria there. We go to philosophy and we find some criteria. We start looking for first principles, and we start asking, "What am I supposed to do?"

Well, all of these things can be and have been identified as fairly arbitrary. Why should anybody tell anybody else what to do? Why should any system compromise the integrity of the individual? Christianity says, "That's the problem, that's not the solution." That's the problem. That's the disaster. We've lost our way.

Only one way is not arbitrary—that is God's way. If you're entering into the Christian tradition, you apprentice yourself, you're catechized. The whole notion of catechesis is borrowed from the guilds, from training people for specific roles. When you were born in the ancient world, you were born into a specific role. If you wanted to pursue a particular course of action, a particular kind of job, you went and apprenticed yourself. In catechesis, you get some master who has worked through the meaning and the vocabulary of the faith, so that you are formed and framed in the right use and handling of that vocabulary. You are part of a particular story, which gives a way of understanding the right relationship between things.

What we've done is to mix up the stories by trying to bring categories from other traditions to bear. The basic question is whose are you? What purpose do you serve? And once you recognize that, the rest of it begins to fall in place.

Question: It's not just a conflict of a religious tradition and a secular one, philosophical tradition or medical tradition, but there are conflicts of traditions within the Christian faith. And what you were getting at about autonomy is a very important concept. That's why we have local movements like communitarian movements trying to bring politics and social thinking back to a community level.

I understood what you were saying. However, it was not intelligible to me in any way.

I grew up on a farm. I had a very pastoral upbringing. I used to wander around with the animals, cutting thistles in the hillside, making up songs to sing to God. And my grandmother, who was on the next hill would say, "Oh, I heard you singing the other day. It was nice." Every Friday, all of the kids in the group were taken down to a church where we had Bible stories. So I have always perceived myself in the context of biblical storytelling and I've never had any sense of myself, throughout fifteen years of a relationship with the same man, in any other way. I see myself in some biblical sense. I really do. Because it's been there since very early.

I'm not asking for same-sex unions to be called marriage or the same as marriage, but I would suggest we discuss them as vocations to which some of us are called. I would further suggest that such unions be called vocations in Christian faith, because they help and support those who are giving glory to God. I really perceive my relationship as something that helps me give glory to God in real and practical ways.

I don't see myself as some abstraction or perceiving my autonomous self, although we all do that to some degree. But I do agree that the church must make a radical stand against rampant individualism for community. I would like to know if either you or Diane Knippers are prepared to acknowledge that the rampant economic individualism is really a much graver moral crime in our society than homosexuality, where people pursue their economic goals, regardless of whether a company hires and fires people based on their sexual orientation or abuses them in some other way.

STANTON: No question. There's a world out there crying for ministry and witness and healing and community and conversion, precisely conversion. This debate in our church is consuming too much of our energy, our time, and our best efforts. We ought to be on to that larger business of mission.

However, I would say that also is part of the basic pattern that I'm trying to identify. I want to affirm you and offering of your gifts to God and glorifying God, but you said the key thing there, "I really perceive." And the whole issue of the biblical pattern, I would submit to you, is that the larger picture is one of surrender. There is no true "self" I can present to God. My true "self" is in God—in Paul's word, "Your life lies hid with Christ in God." (Colossians 3:3) I'm alienated from it by own interest in myself. When Paul says, "I don't want a righteousness of my own," that's a similar emphasis. (Philippians 3:9) But one in Christ. Christ righteousness. I have to learn life all over again. I have to be made a new creature.

When, for example, Paul says there's no longer any Jew nor Greek, slave nor free, male nor female—he's subverting all natural relationships. (Galatians 3:28) But he's also subverting our tendency to identify ourselves in terms of those relationships that grow out of our natural life.

I do not stand before God as a gay or a straight, heterosexual or homosexual. And when I begin to identify myself that way that's part of the whole process of turning away from God, it's part of the story.

I would challenge you to listen to the stories you hear being told and ask: What is the purpose? What is going on here? What is the structure of the story?

If there's a gospel opportunity, it may be that we will, once again, rediscover the essential pattern of the gospel story. I announce to you God's word, not because I have any special insight into it, but because I have known it and it has shaped me. It has changed my life. I announce it to you. I cannot force you to change. But if I announce God's word to you, know this, that word is intended to help you, to free you. It's not the law against, against, against. If we lived only by the law, we'd never get out of this problem either.

What God is calling you to is a radical surrender first, to abandoning the self. We're going to have to do it one of these days: everyone of us in this room is going to die. We're going to have to make a choice to give up everything we have, everything we think we are, all claim to ourselves, and then we will stand and be remade by God.

And that's all that God is asking, all along in the course of this life, the giving of myself, the giving up of all claim to myself and trusting his righteousness and finding my righteousness in him, not in me. "There is neither Greek, nor Jew, slave, free, male or female." I find that to be a very powerful argument against racism, against the diminishing of women and their ministries in the church. I've argued for years that the reason women may be ordained is because we are baptized into Christ; our righteousness is in him, not in ourselves, not in our own self-identity, not in solidarity with others, but only in right relationship with God. Therefore, if I am baptized in Christ, I am a new creature and gender doesn't matter, but behavior does.

"From the beginning, God made them male and female." (Mark 10:6) Human beings are already in that specific kind of relationship. Alienation enters in after the fall, after sin, after the human being begins to serve the self. And the very specific kind of relationship entailed in the story is a relationship that is between the male and the female. Marriage is built into our very physical character. We abstract ourselves out of that and say, "Well, that's not true of me."

And therein lies the seduction.

CHAPTER 4

GOD LOVES YOU
Finding a Common Ground

by LOUIE CREW

Louie Crew is the founder of Integrity, the lesbigay justice ministry of Episcopalians. He was born in Alabama in 1936 and since 1974 has been the life partner of Ernest Clay. Dr. Crew is a member of the Standing Committee of the Diocese of Newark, a frequent deputy to General Convention, and Secretary of the Standing Commission on Anglican and International Peace with Justice Concerns He is a graduate of Baylor (B.A., 1958), Auburn (M.A., 1959), and the University of Alabama (Ph.D., 1971).

Dr. Crew is a Professor of English at Rutgers, the State University of New Jersey, where he chairs the Rutgers University Senate and serves on the Board of Governors. He is the author of over 1,240 publications and the editor of A Book of Revelations: Lesbian and Gay Episcopalians Tell Their Own Stories *(1991).*

A nationally known leader in the movement for gay rights, Crew says, describing his mission, "I would never have chosen to face the difficulties that life has thrust upon me as a sexual outsider; but I choose to respect my survival, so intimately does our character integrate with the obstacles which shape us. Folks have us sexual reformers all wrong: we are less about the business of sensuality than is the neighborhood gossip; ours is the task of all others fed on locusts and wild honey: to make way for the truth."

A friend tells me the story of a lady in New York who was reading about Mother Theresa. Knowing she had a sabbatical coming up, she wrote Mother Theresa a letter, saying, "I want to come to India, to bring my resources with me and work with the poor."

She sent off the letter with a check. She waited for week after week. Her sabbatical got nearer and nearer and she hadn't heard a word until a ratty little envelope with a stamp of India on it arrived. She opened the letter with great expectations and pulled out a tattered sheet of paper. On it were two words: "South Bronx."

I come to say to you today, two words: "Gay Virginia." I'm told that you have 185 parishes in this diocese. I brought a copy of the *Gay Yellowpages*; there are 179 entries for Virginia.

How are you getting across to the people in those institutions that God loves your gay and lesbian neighbor as much as God loves you?

You know, it's so much easier to love our neighbors if we can just pick and choose. But I want you to know, there's no such thing as any condition, not a single condition, that is not a gospel opportunity.

My *husband and I,* and I don't use that term to offend you— it's the only term that says what we call each other, we're both husbands—my husband and I took a break ten years ago, about fourteen years into our marriage, and had a wonderful opportunity to work in Asia for four years.

I remember the first time we walked down a street in Canton. We must have been a sight to see. Two left-handed people. One black, one white, gawking at dogs hanging like turkeys. And we thought, the first one we saw, "Ah, we've heard they eat Rover in China." And so we watched the one fast-food Rover stand until we went to the next one and we went to the next one and we were gawking and they were gawking at us.

We both confessed in the morning, when we got up, that dogs were chasing us in our dreams. And we wrote to my mother-in-law, his mother, in Georgia, and told her about it. She wrote us a wonderful letter back, saying, "Don't you be eatin' any dog, 'lessn you'll be chasing cars." I never did eat Rover yet. I just can't. It's taboo.

The earliest memory I have of a taboo that got to me that deeply was the taboo against homosexuality. I remember going with a friend to the Cherry Lane Theater in New York's Greenwich Village to see *Guys and Dolls*. We walked into the bar next door and there were these men holding hands with each other! I mean, I knew what my body had been telling me since puberty, but I had no idea that people actually ever acted on those feelings without being struck with lightning. I went into the alleyway outside the theater and vomited—I was so afraid.

It was a tremendous taboo. I waited 28 years before I had sex with anybody. When I entered in "the gay life," it wasn't very gay. I thought it was sinful, but I went into it because I finally gave up trying all the other cures. And, for several years, I wandered into some behavior with strangers that I consider quite sinful, because strangers were the only ones with whom I dared risk any kind of assignation.

I thought I had left God, because I thought God had left me. And then this strange thing happened—I met a man. He likes me to tell you that we met at the shopping mall outside Lenox Square, but we actually met in the YMCA, not at Lenox Square, next to the bathroom on the seventh floor. Not a very nice place. And I hadn't been a very nice fellow all weekend. It had been a promiscuous weekend.

Even though I thought he was a cop, I went when he invited me to his room. And I've never left that room. We courted for six months. To begin our relationship, we used the 1928 Book of Common Prayer.

And things started happening that I couldn't account for, a recovery not of my autonomous self, but of my Christian self. I wrote to my parents, because I've always been one to tell the truth. My father and mother, bless their hearts, could understand the sexuality, which was hard enough, more than they could the race difference.

They wrote back, "Well, we hope you won't come see us together because we're retired now and we have to live here. And we think all of our friends will remain good to us, but we're not sure and we don't think it's fair to put them through that."

And I said to Ernest, "Well, get in the car, we're going."

And he said, "What do you mean, didn't you read the letter?"

I said, "Yes, but they're my parents, I know them. They'll love you when they get to know you. You're just like mother anyway."

"No, I'm not going," he said. "I didn't marry them, I married you. And in the first place, I already have the best part. Because you couldn't love me if they hadn't loved you."

I argued and I fussed and I fumed, but I couldn't get him to go. He finally said, "It's only 250 miles. Get on over there and go see them."

But within a very short time, five or six months, my father said to me, "Son, I don't understand it. You have to forgive me. I was born in 1905 in the poorest county of Alabama. I can't understand how a son of mine could love a negra as an equal. And so I've been worried. I thought maybe you felt inferior and loved him thinking you weren't good enough. That would be so unhealthy. But I can't find any evidence for that. Then I thought maybe you thought he was superior. And that would be unhealthy. And I don't see any evidence for that."

And then he said, "There's something, son, you won't understand, because you'll never be a father, but I watched you from the day you were born, I've watched the way you smile. I see your mother's smile; I see my smile. I watched the way you learned to walk. I've loved you. But there's always been something about you that's very tentative and I haven't been able to put my finger on it. But, since you've been with that man, that's no longer there. You have to go home and tell him, I can't meet him yet, but you have to tell him one thing—I have to love him because he's given me my son back, whole."

There are many gay people who can't say that. I'm blessed. You see, when St. Peter was on that rooftop in Joffa, there was just nothing more disgusting than dog, there was just nothing more disgusting than pigs' feet. And furthermore, he could have said, "Well Jesus didn't say we're supposed to do that. And 3,000 years of tradition didn't say that. And reason doesn't say that. And how in the world can this vision come and say, 'We're going to change?' The vision doesn't have Scripture, tradition or reason on its side."

And the voice said, "Call not unclean anyone whom I have made."

I believe that God is alive, that God is still speaking, and God has spoken to me. Things started happening in my relationship that I could not account for.

I'm not talking about loving somebody when he's nice. I'm talking about loving somebody when he's *not* nice. And I'm not talking about somebody loving me when I'm nice. I'm talking about somebody loving me when I am not nice. I never had met any person in my life who could love me when I'd been my worst self. Even my parents couldn't come around to doing that very well.

Sex has not been our besetting sin. I wish I could tell you it was. Sex is so easy. Our besetting sin has not been a temptation to unfaithfulness—our sins are much more ordinary and ugly, like pride, and selfishness, and unkindness.

Remember that the gospel has some very precious and delicate moments. Let's rehearse some of them. Don't rewrite the gospel. When Jesus is hanging there at Calvary and the thief says to him, "Well, you've been pretty badly treated. I deserve what I got. Remember me when you get into heaven." Jesus did *not* say, "What are you talking about? You want cheap grace? Are you sure that you've thoroughly repented? Can you say that a little louder, I can't hear that over here. And furthermore, there's somebody down there writing it all down. I want to be sure it's in the book."

He didn't turn to the Samaritan woman and say she was a sinner. He teased her. He did not deal with her about her sin. He dealt with her about her thirst.

The father of the Prodigal Son did not say, "All right. Come on in here, prodigal. I want you to know that your brother is going to get all of my money, because he's the one who stayed and was faithful. We're going to take you back into this house, but you're going to have to stay in the back bedroom and you're going to have to clean up after your elder brother and we'll give you chicken dinner. But no veal scaloppine for you."

That's not the way the stories are told. But that is the way the stories are retold to my community.

A friend of mine, who spends his summers as a priest on Fire Island, was at a fund raiser last summer for the Lambda Legal Defense Fund there. He said, "I was a little fashionable. I had my little flowing priestly garment and my white collar on. And I went to the cocktail party, a cocktail party to die for." (We sisters can be so grand when we're trying to prove to somebody we're worth something!)

During the party, a young man and his lover came up to him and pointed to his collar and said, "Jesus kills," and walked away. That's not what Jesus does, but that's what they've been hearing in the gay and lesbian community.

When I was at Baylor, I went to see a psychiatrist. And this guy got me to start dating a woman named Bobbie Jean. I would go back regularly and tell the psychiatrist what progress I was making on this journey towards heterosexuality. I remember how awkward it was, even to try to hold hands. And one night she kissed me. So I kissed her back. Of course, the psychiatrist was just in heaven when I told him about that. And then I asked him, "Shouldn't I tell her?"

"Tell her what?" he asked.

"Well, shouldn't I tell her about all these feelings I'm really having which aren't about her?"

"Oh, no! Don't tell her. That would make it not work. It'll work well enough if you'll just go along with it." But there was just something so fundamentally wrong about that.

If we are honest, I would suspect that all of us know some-body who's been in a marriage that should never have taken place, a marriage that would not have taken place if there had been honesty, candor, and safety. Sex is not of a whole lot of importance, and yet it's very important, it's integral. It doesn't define a relationship. How many minutes a month does it take? Yet it's integral to who you are. And certainly your son or your daughter has a right to be in a relationship with somebody who's attracted to him or her and not imagining somebody else. I'm not talking about a right to sexuality; I'm talking about the right to be a human being. And while your sexuality is not a means of grace, marriage is. It's a sacrament.

Noel Coward wrote a play, *Just a Song at Twilight,* about Somerset Maugham, in which Maugham is near the end of his life and his family finds out that he is gay. Everybody else knew, but he didn't think his family did. They confront him with the fact that they know he's gay. It's the moment Maugham has been terrified of all of his life. And he finds out that they're angry with him, not because he's gay, but because he didn't love them enough to share that with them. There are probably many people in your life that may not find you safe enough to share that either.

* * *

Six years into our marriage, my father called and said, "I want to speak to my son, please."

I said, "Dad, this is your son."

He said, "No Louie, I want to speak to my other son."

My father said to Ernest, "Lula and I aren't very happy with the way we've lived towards you. And we want you to come to our home. I know it's not fair to put that kind of pressure on you, but would you come?"

Ernest said, "Yes." And when we went, they invited all their closest circle of friends to come.

The town had already known. They'd seen me on television. When I was on Atlanta television, they'd go over to my parents' house to be sure they weren't watching.

And I remember being with my father the last time. He was in the nursing home and he had dwindled down to 90 pounds, trying to starve himself to death, since there was almost no other way to deal with his wracking pain.

I said to him, "Dad, I know I'm not the son that you wanted. But I love you very much. Remember those times when you'd vote against the majority so the Baptists couldn't have it unanimous? And I'd be so embarrassed.

"You have no idea how important that's been to me. I've lived in a world where I know that the world doesn't fall apart when you don't agree with everybody else. Because it didn't fall apart when you disagreed with everybody. And I thank you."

And he got very angry, very worked up. He pulled himself up to the side of the bed. After several minutes, he got himself so he looked at me eye to eye and said, "Oh, Louie, you're so wrong. You are the son that I wanted. And I love you very much."

That was my dad. He died. But my father, our father, wants to say the same thing to each one of you with this gospel opportunity, and I'm sure that's why I'm on this planet—God wants you! God wants you!

There are thousands of people who will never hear God loves them if I don't tell them that. And don't you ever tell them that until you know how much God loves you. Because that's the only way that you can keep saying it.

I'm not here to proclaim my goodness. I don't know that God is present in my relationship because of how good we are. It sure wouldn't measure very well if that were necessary. I know God is present in my relationship because God is good. God loves you.

Can we live with our theological differences and find a way to say that together? You know, the whole world is waiting for us to get over this issue, so we can get on with the bigger issue, which is God loves the whole world.

Q&A

Question: You say that Jesus didn't say anything about food before he was crucified, so Peter had neither Scripture or reason for guidance. But in Mark, Chapter 7, when Jesus is challenged over some ritual things having to do with food and handwashing, he makes a fairly trenchant comment to the people who were haranguing him. And Mark says, "Therefore, Jesus declared that all foods were clean." And so it seems to me that what was happening on the roof at Joffa was that Peter was catching up with the Scripture and with the tradition.

CREW: I would agree with you. But I think a lot of other people were with him in catching up. I don't think he was the only holdout. I think he was a part of the majority. I think you've got some antecedents for what I'm asking about lesbian and gay people too.

And John McNeill, the Jesuit scholar who wrote *The Church and the Homosexual,* often preaches on that wonderful prayer which we take very seriously in my Anglo-Catholic parish, "O

Lord, I'm not worthy to come under thy roof, but speak the word only and *my soul,*" we say, "shall be healed." That could very likely be *my lover* shall be healed. The text does allow that possible gloss. Certainly it might explain why the Roman didn't want that Jew to come anywhere near to see who was really over there, but he's got these miraculous powers. So, "I'm not worthy," that you should come see who I'm asking you to bless. But if you've got this power, do it.

But I'm also reading, I think, with the power of the Spirit. And if it doesn't work for you, can we still go on for what does work for you? I have nothing at stake trying to prove that particular text to mean that thing. But I do think that's what we're doing—that's what you're doing for Peter in hindsight. And I would just like to ask doing it for lesbians and gays as well.

Question: [Tearful] I want to apologize for myself and every other heterosexual who finds it so easy because we fit in. I ask your forgiveness.

CREW: I thank you. But let me assure you, your forgiveness was there at Calvary, long before I came here. It's the only source of any forgiveness and you certainly have mine. And you have Jesus'.

I hear this so often. I got a letter by e-mail a year or so ago from somebody saying, "Are you the same Louie Crew that used to live in Fort Valley with a black lover?"

He went on to say, "I thought I'd never get a chance to see you or contact you. I grew up in Fort Valley and was one of the boys that used to come and throw rocks at your apartment. My family encouraged us. We would call and say we were going to murder you.

"I thought I'd never get a chance to apologize. See, because I grew up gay. You don't know how much it meant to me to know that you survived the worst we could give you." He said, "Will you forgive me?"

How can I not forgive him? That's what grace is all about.

I'm not going to go up to heaven and say, "Let me in, I'm gay." I'm not going to go up and say anything except, "Lord, have mercy on me, a sinner." You got a better deal? That's the best deal I know, because I know I can go in that way. I'm frightened by the judgment day, but I'm not nearly as frightened by the judgment day as I am about some of the ones who are trying to preempt the Lord and do it now.

Question: Listening to your story moved me—it made me laugh, it made me cry. And when I listened to the man who spoke last night, his story was heart-wrenching and moving and invoked many feelings.

On the other hand, people speaking against acceptance of homosexuality speak more to my mind. They have a value there they are trying to uphold, which was a place for the law and that meant something to them. The question is, why is there this polarity in the presentation style of both sides—feeling versus intellect and how do we bring all this together and come back to a walk with the Lord where we are supposed to be offering ourselves to the Lord?

CREW: I can assure you I'm not a professor at Rutgers University on the basis of my feelings. When I'm called to a forum like this, I don't get to leave the position I present when it's over. I envy so much Bishop Lee's comment about doing this for only an hour a day. I do this 100 percent of the day. Because even when Samaritans are out there taking you out of the ditch and putting you in the hospital, they're still Samaritans doing it. In other words, there's no escape. So my story must not be the intellectual one for you. The intellectual basis is there. You heard it last night from Gray Temple. I'm not here just to make a point. I'm here to be incarnating what we're talking about. But I hope that does not include throwing out the brain.

I think there will be taboos about this for an awfully long time. But you've got to go right on loving. And even if you're going to determine that it is theologically wrong, God says that you've got to love those that are least among you, and that's how you're going to get into heaven. I have to love you. I really do believe that Summary of the Law. I'm going to be judged by how much I can love the ones who disagree with me. I didn't come here just to convert you. I've got to love you when I can't convert you.

It's not my job to convert you. That's God's. Mine is just to tell my story.

Panel Discussion

*(In this segment of the Conference, Bishop Lee reads
questions that have been submitted by the audience.)*

LEE: Bishop Stanton, Gray Temple made reference to the
"selective exegesis" employed by fundamentalists and others
who condemn homosexual behavior on biblical grounds. Is
there a responsible way to interpret and apply Leviticus and
Romans to this issue, without being selective?

STANTON: Yes. In fact, this became clear to me as I was grap-
pling toward a way to talk about the tradition or the pattern. It's
interesting to me that Jesus doesn't deny the law. He takes, for
example, the Second Commandment: "Thou shalt love thy
neighbor as thyself," from Leviticus, Chapter 19. It falls right in
the middle of the section having to do with sexuality. Clearly,
Jesus knew the law, and when he says something like, "Not one
dot, not one tittle of the law will pass away," he's conversant with
it. He's read it. He's studied it. It's part of the pattern of his life.

And it's part of the pattern he enjoins upon his disciples.

Now this is not to say that Jesus is teaching that if you obey
the law, if you do everything the law tells you to do, you will, in
fact, be saved. That's the problem with the Pharisees. And what
happens with the Pharisees is not that they're legalistic, but that
their legalism takes a particular course.

In the matter of divorce, the Pharisees have a question
about when is it right to divorce. They begin to get into word
studies; they begin to get into hermeneutics. They even have
dialogues to get at the theological issue: When is it all right to
divorce? They move progressively away from the law. Shammai

says it has to be for a weighty cause, probably sexual infidelity. Hillel says for any reason at all. Guess which was the most popular movement in that time. The Pharisaical movement of Hillel was the larger.[9]

Jesus goes in the opposite direction. He ratchets it up. He confronts the people with their sin, with the law, and purports to interpret it in a way that the law has never been interpreted, in a very strict way. Why?

The pattern is to assault our sense of self, to assault our sense self-sufficiency, to assault our sense that through the use of our mind or reason or tradition or whatever we want to call it, we can move away from God's law, and thus to drive us right to the mercy of God.

Now, I think there's a pattern there, that it is possible to make sense of the law and not get lost in things which, on other grounds, are exempted by Jesus.

TEMPLE: I think there are alternative traditions to that understanding. In the first place, when Jesus said, "Not one dot or tittle will pass from the law," it seems to me by context, he was protecting the written code of the Old Testament against the growing proto-Talmud, the tradition of the elders that, in the Gospel of Matthew particularly, he was implacably opposed to.

And there's another tradition as to what the law is for. It's taken from Exodus 25 and Exodus 40. Moses was instructed to build a box, put the tablets of testimony in the box, build a slab of gold, get seven or eight fellows to take that slab of gold and put it on top, and then God's going to sit on the lid of the thing and do business with his people.

It seems to me that those architectural details tell us that God has put himself between his law and the people. I think he made the tablets of stone so we wouldn't wave them around. He put the heaviest substance then known on top of it, so we couldn't take it out and play with it all the time. He knew that you can no more make yourself good by keeping the law than you can make yourself well when you're sick by eating a stethoscope. The law is a diagnostic device designed to impel us into the presence of the God who gives us the law.

LEE: Gray Temple speaks of discerning God's grace in people, relationships and situations. Do you think God's grace is only present in situations and relationships of which God specifically approves? How is God's grace discerned, both by individuals and by the church? Should the church change its teaching of God's law to approve of all those actions and relationships and situations in which God extends grace?

TEMPLE: My own reading strategy, which I don't ask you to share, but I do ask you to understand, is that the Scripture as God has given it to us is a dynamic process. Those who disagree with me say it's a closed content. Consequently, they speak with comfort about God's will, God's plan, God's law. I feel less comfort with that. I would say the Scriptures, as we have them, catalyze our present access to God's will, God's plan and God's law. I think this is a fundamental epistemological difference.

LEE: How do we encounter the Holy One, through Scripture or through direct discernment?

CREW: I think one of the major reasons we live together in community is so that we can test one another in regard to what we feel is our response to the Spirit. Certainly in the Integrity movement and as a gay Christian, I'm very well aware of the possibility of being deceived. I know. I've seen it happen. I've been deceived enough myself about what I thought was right and found out I was wrong.

We must constantly call ourselves and have others around call us. That's one of the reasons I'm so afraid, frankly, of a straight priest having much to do with gay people—because I'm afraid they won't hold us to a high enough standard. I don't want anybody not holding me to a high standard.

So I think we must not just assume everything's all right, because somebody tells me, "My spirit tells me it's all right."

That must be held up to accountable standards within our community of discernment, not individual discernment.

STANTON: Discernment is one of the words that takes its meaning from the tradition in which it participates. You learn the ability to discern by being grounded in a tradition. I believe that the Christian tradition says that discernment is the outcome of having first been submitted to a way of looking at the world. That first submission is to know that God is not here to affirm me, but I am here to give everything to God—to deny myself in the words of Jesus—which is why the law becomes important. Discernment is a thing that comes out of the ability, having been submitted, to begin to recognize the right proportion of things. This is true in every tradition.

Obviously, there are other different traditions. What I'm saying is that any other tradition supplanting this one, is supplanting the Christian one. I would like to be criticized in terms of the Christian tradition. That does not mean I need to be told that there are other traditions. That's part of the problem.

If God speaks, has he declared his word? The word of the Bible is "God's word." Now, that's not *sola scriptura*. But that tradition interprets itself, defines itself, guides itself, in discernment. As you acquire, through humility, the submission and skills you begin to see how it fits together in proportion.

If it can be critiqued from within, that is great. I would propose you critique every tradition from within its own terms to see where it leads. That, I think, is one way, at least, of getting at the truth. But the question is, if God has spoken, where is it? The Bible claims it is spoken there, that God has spoken there and that those who follow that pattern come to understand that.

LEE: Why does strengthening the family mutually exclude any possibility of also affirming wholesome, life-long, same-sex relationships? And, related to that, what would you say to gay and lesbian couples who are raising their children in this church, whose children are also gifts of God and baptized in this church.

KNIPPERS: One of the things that I think should always be the goal of an occasion like this is to achieve disagreement. Because, so often in these debates, we're just talking past each other. And one of the points at which I'd like to try to achieve disagreement is this question of identity.

I would say to gay or lesbian couples who are rearing children who are baptized in the Episcopal Church—God loves you. God loves those children. They are precious children of the church and precious children of God. But I think a part of expressing love is telling the truth. What I don't understand is the perception difference between what I say to my straight friends and what I say to my homosexual friends. Which is, to all of them, God loves you, and he has a certain plan for the expression of sexuality.

I have three friends who are with us here this weekend. One is a single woman who has never been married, one is a divorced man, and one is a woman who is legally separated from her husband. They know I love them. And a part of my love is to say, "It is God's plan for you to abstain from genital sexual expression." And that's the same message that I'm trying to convey to my homosexual friends.

LEE: Say a word about the distinction between heterosexual and homosexual marriage. Should the latter actually be called marriage? Is it naive to have the blessing of same-sex unions and not call it marriage?

CREW: I'm not sure I know enough about heterosexual marriage, though it's pretty much ubiquitous, to make a comparison. Diane made reference to the conference in Pasadena where gay and lesbian people were considering entering relationships without pledges to life-long unions. I was at that conference and I spoke to keep the 1928 Prayer Book requirement of that pledge. That's been a very important pledge for Ernest and me to have made to each other. And I really do believe that the sacramental nature of marriage is such that it's realized much more when things are not going well than when things are.

And so I also do agree with you, that it's silly not to call it marriage. It's marriage and let's call it marriage.

TEMPLE: I think the most fruitful passage of Scripture to study with regard to marriage is probably First Corinthians, Chapter 7. If you study that passage, St. Paul posits what I take to be four values which characterize godly marriage.

The first is fidelity to each other. The second is truthfulness with each other. The third is mutuality so that there is not a power imbalance. And the fourth is permanence. I think that's descriptive and I'm comfortable with that being definitive of what God wants us to understand marriage as being. I'm sounding now like a "Scripture as a closed-content person," but I'd be happy with that content. What Louie and I and our colleagues are pleading for is that the sexual covenant with Almighty God that that passage describes be extended to every Christian so that we are able to offer these values to gay Christians as well as to straight and, as Louie pleads, hold people both accountable and to offer them the support necessary to live that quality of commitment, faithfulness, truthfulness, mutuality and permanence. Gay people are as capable of that as straight people. St. Paul never says a word to connect marriage with childbirth and so when we do, as part of the *bene esse* of marriage, we go outside of the Christian tradition, or at least the New Testament tradition.

STANTON: I would question that. St. Paul, being a good Pharisee, would understand and grasp what was meant by, "Be fruitful and multiply," as a command in the tradition. But let me suggest to both of you that your position is incoherent. If life-long unions are to be expected of gay marriages, they can only be seen in terms of the analysis that's being used on heterosexual marriage, and as arbitrary in one degree or another. Why do you choose life-long union? The very people who have argued most against this are the people who say that homosexuality is different than heterosexuality and that heterosexual standards ought not apply.

They say, "Your position on life-long union is arbitrary."

Now you say, "But it serves certain useful purposes."

Does it? Your critique of heterosexual marriage is, "My God, we've got all kinds of messes all over this world. We've got to help people learn to manage the difficulties in their marriages." They've already made that life-long pledge. And yet, we seem to deal with that in a very different way. We seem to say, "Well, if the marriage dies, you just give it up."

It's incoherent. It doesn't work. You're using a text out of St. Paul to suggest, for example, that we ought to have four categories. Why four? What is mutuality? What are these values? And doesn't the whole concept of value presuppose that the final decision for that rests in me? I make value choices. God gives commandments. God gives the objective reality into which I'm entering.

If you want it interpreted that way, I'll interpret it that way from Paul. But then you're violating your own principle by seeing it closed.

So, the point I want to make is that the way you're using the tradition to limit a category fails because it's already been rendered inapplicable by many who argue these same things.

KNIPPERS: I was looking at the list Gray cited: fidelity, truthfulness, mutuality and permanence. I hope those characterize many, many relationships that I have. I hope that they characterize my relationship with my church. I hope they characterize my relationship with every member of my family. There are friendships that those words characterize.

It seems to me that, in the end, this definition of marriage being mutual aid and comfort is something that applies to lots of different relationships. It's not unique to marriage. It strikes me as a Gnostic approach, because part of marriage, what's intrinsic to marriage, is physical. It's body. It's incarnational.

That's consistent with the incarnational faith we have. We can't get away from the body and the blood—the physical body, the death, the resurrection, the celebration of the Eucharist, and we just keep wanting to flee from that. And, a part of marriage, as it was instituted at the very first marriage when men and women were created, is very physical and has to do with the complementarity between a male body and female body.

LEE: How do we as a church embrace the homosexual unabashedly, without promoting a promiscuous and life-threatening lifestyle? In blessing same-sex unions are we, as a church, condemning these persons to a shorter life?

CREW: I'm glad to hear people asking the question, because I think it's important: How do you move within the community that I'm inviting you to move in and still remain faithful to your own perspective of what is right and wrong?

I think the best model for me is Jesus. Jesus was known as a friend of sinners. I'm not very expert on good people, but, being one, I know a lot about sinners. And you don't get to be my friend, you don't get invited back to my house by coming in my house and insulting me.

You know, the real test is not whom you invite to dinner, but whether the sinner invites you. And if you're considered a friend, you're invited back. Jesus was invited back. He did not have a reputation as a friend of ex-drunkards. He was a friend of drunkards. Nor did he have a reputation as a friend of ex-prostitutes. They condemned him as being a friend of prostitutes.

My suggestion is that we ought not to try to upstage judgment day. It's God's. My job is to love the world, not to judge it. And I've seen people do this in the heterosexual world with kids at college, I've seen chaplains move in and help out when the pregnancy happened that wasn't supposed to happen, and they moved in lovingly and unjudgmentally, not as the judge that was feared.

Most of the gay people that I know who are living in obviously broken ways don't know that we're there to love them. So I think that's where we start.

TEMPLE: How many priests here have ever excommunicated parishioners for adultery? I see that there are about four of us.

Those of us who raised our hands can, I think, partially answer that question. The advantage to bringing homosexuals under the rest of the covenant that we enjoy—whether it's the '28 or '79 Prayer Book—is that you now have a public covenant that they've sworn to before God and the church. And you can go to them and appeal to them on the basis of that discipline.

And if they subsequently say that's not the church's business, I am by nature promiscuous, I get to say, "I am also by nature promiscuous, and by God's grace, and debt of my oath and the church's support and accountability, I don't fool around, and you are called to repentance." I think it's way past time that the church extend this protection and this accountability to all of our people and not just those of us who are in married relationships.

STANTON: That seems to me an incoherent position to say, "Let's make homosexual relationships permanent so that if they don't become permanent, we have a basis on which to excommunicate them and they can choose some other lifestyle." That's a use of law that seems entirely arbitrary to me.

TEMPLE: I think that to excommunicate someone who's in violation of their marriage vows is not arbitrary or subjective. It surprises me to hear a bishop take that position.

STANTON: The place where I find it arbitrary is to the argument that motivates making relationships—homosexual relationships—into marriage, then allows you to excommunicate them if they violate the life-long union. Why do you apply the life-long union commitment to the homosexual relationship. Your answer was, because that gives us some way of disciplining people, and I would say that's a use of power, and that's an arbitrary use of power. Arbitrary in the sense that there's no internal judgment or justification for the use of that kind of power.

TEMPLE: If they stand before the church and we solemnize particular vows that they hold themselves accountable to, we are then taking them seriously.

STANTON: I hear someone saying, "Why would I want to do that if that's what you want to use that rule for? Why would I want to do that?"

TEMPLE: I think that would be an excellent question and we should ask that for every couple. I, for example, don't perform weddings where there's a pre-nuptial agreement. I don't want them flying with parachutes.

CREW: I do feel an obligation to point out something else that is, I think, related to the point I was trying to make about taboo. I've said more than enough about my own commitment and my relationship, but I think the church does sometimes want to get us married so they get away from some issues that the church still must deal with.

There's a great deal about sexuality among heterosexuals that's not in marriage. It's called courtship. And I do think the church must be a safe place for people to express affection and be obvious about their love. One of the major ways I can cause an accident is just simply by kissing Ernest when I'm leaving to go to the airport. In fact, we don't do it. In the darkness of the theater we might hold hands. But mostly we don't, because it just causes heterosexuals to go into conniptions.

There's a whole level of erotics that you just take for granted among heterosexuals that homosexuals are not allowed. So that it may sometimes seem convenient if you can get them married without any courtship and stick them off in a bedroom somewhere and say that they're blessed and be done with it. I think we must be honest and admit that lots of people go through several crushes before they fall permanently in love with somebody. We need a place where it's safe for homosexuals to be erotic in the church on a par with heterosexuals.

LEE: The language of sexual intimacy and the language or spiritual union overlap, yet the realities they point to are different. I am hearing a confusion at this level. Those who claim that life-giving, same-sex love adds a spiritual dimension and assume that this implies God's pleasure, but God's grace and God's approval are not synonymous. Could you please comment?

CREW: It's a faith statement, isn't it? I don't know how you go anywhere with that. It seems to me that it's obvious that God's approval is not necessarily on all of us. Even St. Paul, who seemed to have a lot of answers, was willing to say, "I, right now, see only through the dark glass," even about very basic things like faith.

But I do know that the relative value of faith is very little compared to the relative value of love. Almost all I've heard about faith in this discussion has been that faith is somehow our gift to God. I don't see faith that way at all. I see faith as God's gift to me. It is a spiritual gift and I have no idea why I have so much of it. Nor does it make me better than others. I know many people who have almost no faith at all, who live more faithfully than I do. But I'm enormously grateful for the faith.

How many of you in this room have not always, since youth, or babyhood, been Episcopalians? More than half of us. Maybe it's not true for you, but it's certainly true for many converts I know—one of the reasons people come into the Episcopal Church is because we don't require lie detectors at the Creed. We don't ask you to hang up your brain at the door. When I joined this church I wasn't even sure if I believed in God. That didn't make any difference—God believed in me. God believes in us. It's God's love of us that this church is about, not how we make God happen because we are theologically correct.

I'm not trying to discount those faith questions, I think we should ask them. And I think it's a continuing process. But let's honor the fact that we are still in the dark and God is the light.

TEMPLE: I want to observe that the question that we were originally responding to seems to arise from one of the epistemologies that we've been talking about. The question of distinguishing between God's grace and God's approval assumes that the Scripture is a closed content, a compendium of all Christian truth.

And, I simply want to make another forlorn plea for the fact that there are those of us who have found that, in a late-modernist epistemology, God can be discovered, God can be known, God can be loved, God can be worshiped, God can be obeyed, God can be served, and God can be recommended to others.

One does not have to pretend to a pre-modernist biblical epistemology in order to house God. God will bring God's self up, whatever our epistemology is.

LEE: This is addressed to Bishop Stanton and Diane Knippers. Suppose that sometime in the next five or ten years hard proof is produced that homosexual orientation is at least partially genetically determined; would this event force any change in your theological analysis?

STANTON: The claim is often made that sexual orientation is determined biologically either through the genes, hormonal or pre-natal hormonalization, or brain function and so forth. Science today says that it doesn't look like it.

I can cite you example after example, but the basic issue is that the geneticists, Robert Lewontin, for example, says there is no possibility, there is no way for the genes to discretely influence behaviors.[10]

But let's imagine there was such a discovery. Would it make a difference? No. And here's the reason. The argument that has been offered for natural law is that because we are male and female, because we have differing and complementary genitalia, we therefore, are meant to marry. And rightly, the criticism has been you can't argue from is to what ought to be. But if you can't argue from is to ought in the traditional way, then you can't argue from is to ought in a post-modern way, namely, you go from the fact that people seem to be born with a homosexual orientation and then argue that it ought to be affirmed.

John Money lists some 52 paraphilias, deeply rooted orientations.[11] Now, if all of them are genetic, if they're biological, how in the world do you close the door on some? That is a case of arbitrariness. If you're going from what is, what science purportedly shows us what is, to what ought to be, you are necessarily involved in a fairly slippery application.

The Scripture, the tradition out of which I have been formed, says God intends a certain kind of relationship, namely marriage. It was the new creation.

KNIPPERS: What if we did discover homosexuality was genetically determined? I'm here to tell you that it was not genetically determined that I be monogamous, that does not come naturally for me. I suspect there are many people in the room that could say the same thing. So that a part of our Christian lot is learning how to control some things that may be genetic or that come naturally to us.

I know a lot of people who want to get this behind us so we can get on with the mission of the church. I think this is the mission of the church right now. In every generation, the church has been confronted by difficult and challenging questions. And often those are difficult and challenging questions within the context of the larger culture.

CREW: I would caution us against the possibility of turning sexuality of any sort into idolatry. And particularly, it seems to me, heterosexuals run the risk of doing that. We do too. For the moment I may speak that way, especially by using Scripture to do it. Jesus did not get married. St. Paul said, "Don't do it unless you're burning." But, we are in a community where all of these icons of marriage are based on very slim numbers of text, and are not central to that story.

LEE: Where do we go from here? Can we express our mission without resolving this issue one way or the other?

CREW: We have to. I think we have to go on expressing our mission. I believe that our mission is to love God with our heart, mind, soul and strength and our neighbors as ourselves. What does God require of us but to do justice, love mercy, and walk humbly.

Because of the way this conference is structured, we have to emphasize our differences. But I've heard a lot of things that we have in common. We've got so much to begin talking about. And I don't know that we're going to be able to do that if we have to get all of this issue solved first. But we can go right on loving each other and working through these things. We must! The world needs us.

STANTON: I want to affirm exactly what Louie said. I found much that I could agree with, and much that I think simply needs clarification and working through, and I would covet the opportunity for some group such as this to continue in dialogue. If we can't do it in a small group, I wonder what we can expect in the large. So maybe there's some progress there.

What we're hearing from bishops around the world is, that they don't recognize this kind of solution, namely blessing same-sex unions and ordaining persons living in same-sex unions, as a part of the pattern of the tradition. That's what you're hearing from the church abroad. And certainly, if numbers count, that is the most important segment.

But let us continue to work. I don't see anything against any Christians praying for any other Christians for the strengthening and graces they need to deal with life as it is for them. But that's not the same thing as salvation. And it can't be misrepresented that way, that it's a pattern that is approved of God or is a grace of God. It cannot be. But Christians pray for Christians in questionable situations all the time. Can we move forward that way and not press the agenda? That's the question. If we press the agenda, there will be people who say the pattern is no longer the gospel. That is the threat. We're buying into a different pattern.

TEMPLE: I think the Episcopal Church of the United States is an ideal matrix for this discussion, because we are not a confessional church, but a sacramental one.

The reason Jack Spong and Steve Jetko can receive Communion at the same altar, is because they truly and earnestly repent their sins and are in love and charity with their neighbors and intend to lead a new life following the commandments of God and walking in his holy way. So, they kneel together.

It's not because Steve embraces the Creed as binding, and Jack lives in adult engagement with it—which is a somewhat different posture—it's finally because, on Saturday night, they spend some time with God in silence and kneel together Sunday morning.

If we can maintain the sacramentality of our community, then it seems to me we have broad confessional room for this kind of conversation.

NOTES

1. Robert Wright, *The Moral Animal: Why We Are the Way We Are: The New Science of Evolutionary Psychology* (New York: Vintage Books, 1995).

2. Paul MacLean, *The Triune Brain in Human Evolution: Role in Paleocerebral Functions* (New York: Plenum Publishing, 1990).

3. Doug LeBlanc, "Activists Say Inclusion Is Not Enough," *United Voice,* July 1997.

4. "Marriage in America: A Report to the Nation," Council on Families in America, 1995. (Institute for American Values, 1841 Broadway, Suite 211, New York, NY 10023.)

5. Remarks by Wade Horn, Washington Summit, Ecumenical Coalition on Women and Society, November 1997. (Institute on Religion and Democracy, 1521 16th Street, NW, Suite 300, Washington, DC 20036.)

6. "Marriage In America," op.cit.

7. Carter Heyward, *Touching Our Strength: The Erotic as the Power and the Love of God* (San Francisco: Harper & Row, 1989), p. 109.

8. "Will's Story" in Louie Crew, ed., *A Book of Revelations: Lesbian and Gay Episcopalians Tell Their Own Stories* (Washington, DC: Integrity, Inc., 1991), pp. 10-14.

9. Shammai and Hillel were first-century rabbis, contemporaries of Jesus. It is widely thought that the dispute over divorce, found in Mark 10:1–14 and parallels, was an attempt to draw Jesus into taking the one side or the other. For more on this, see Michael Hilton and Gordan Marshall, *The Gospels & Rabbinic Judaism* (Hoboken: KTAV Publishing House, 1988), pp. 121 ff.; also Jacob Neusner, *Judaism and the Beginning of Christianity* (Philadelphia: Fortress Press, 1984), esp. pp. 81 ff.

10. Robert Lewontin, et al., *Not In Our Genes: Biology, Ideology, and Human Nature* (New York: Pantheon Books, 1984). "We do assert that we cannot think of any significant social behavior that is built into our genes in such a way that it cannot be modified and shaped by social conditioning." p. 267.

11. John Money, *Gay, Straight and In-between: The Sexology of Erotic Orientation* (New York: Oxford University Press, 1988), pp. 126-185.